D0296614

FROM CRABSHACK TO OYSTER BAR

To Tom

FROM CRABSHACK TO OYSTER BAR

EXPLORING SCOTLAND'S SEAFOOD TRAIL

www.theseafoodtrail.com

CAROLE FITZGERALD

with photography by

LAURA THOMSON and ANN KENNEDY

ANGELS' SHARE

The Angels' Share is an imprint of
Neil Wilson Publishing Ltd
The Pentagon Centre
Washington Street
GLASGOW
G3 8AZ

Tel: 0141-221-1117
Fax: 0141-221-5363
E-mail: info@nwp.co.uk
www.nwp.co.uk

© Carole Fitzgerald, 2006
Photographs © Laura Thomson, Ann Kennedy,
Tove Knight and Loch Fyne Oyster Bar 2006
Map on page 3 © Drawing Attention, 2006

The author has asserted her moral right under the
Design, Patents and Copyright Act, 1988, to be
identified as the Author of this Work.

A catalogue record for this book is available from the
British Library.

ISBN 1-903238-81-1
Printed and bound by Oriental Press, Dubai

Picture Credits

Ann Kennedy: 1, 4, 10 (upper right), 14-15, 17, 19-20, 27, 34, 36, 40, 49 (second from bottom), 56, 59, 67, 74, 76 (upper)

Laura Thomson: Front and back cover images, 6, 8-12, 16, 18, 22, 24-6, 29-33, 37-40 (lower right), 41, 43, 45-47, 49, 51-55, 63-66, 68-69

Tove Knight: 58

Loch Fyne Oyster Bar: 71-73, 75-77

CONTENTS

INTRODUCTION

I have always been a 'seafoodie'. As a youngster on holiday in Scotland, I'd clamber over rocks with my dad to find the 'perfect' crab to be thrown into the 'fishpot' for tea that night. Once married, I'd sit for hours on the end of some 'middle-of-nowhere' pier, fishing for mackerel with my husband and son. The weather was always irrelevant and the catch often determined how supper would go that night. On good days, we'd assemble bucket barbecues and eat our fresh-caught feast watching the sun go down. On less clement days we'd dry our wet clothes in front of a fire and grill our mackerel with butter and herbs; a few new potatoes, a good glass of wine to wash it down ... perfect.

Today, following a lifestyle shift from city-based

magazine editor to rural dweller, I own the Anchor Hotel – a pink-façaded beacon in the tiny fishing village of Tarbert, Loch Fyne. From my window each morning I watch the fishing boats head out to sea, never quite sure what's going to be on the menu that night until the boats return to harbour. During the winter, when business is quiet and the days are short, we take our usual meandering route to one of the many wonderful seafood restaurants, hotels or pubs that sprinkle this Argyll coastline. Spoilt for choice, we enjoy whatever the mood takes, and it is these Sunday excursions, along with an abundance of wonderful seafood and shellfish, that inspired the creation of The Seafood Trail. I have never visited any other part of the country that can offer such wonderful seafood and shellfish in such quantity.

Scotland's West Coast is renowned, world-wide, for its spectacular scenery. Regardless of weather or season, the mountains, lochs and islands that litter the landscape attract a growing number of visitors keen to escape normally busy lives in order to explore, unwind and enjoy. Not surprisingly, sampling the locally produced seafood and shellfish has added a whole new dimension to an experience that many believed could not have been bettered.

If you're familiar with this part of the world, you'll know that this was not always the case – remember how difficult it used to be to find restaurants and hotels offering seafood-led menus? If fish was on offer, it was usually battered or beaten, and shellfish generally arrived out of its shell, drowned in pink sauce and hidden on a bed of withered greens. Cookery books reflected this with their old-fashioned design and recipes that were weighted down heavily by rich sauces and high fat content. An emphasis on technique belied the fact that most good butchers and fishmongers could take the hard work out of preparation. Hard to imagine then, Argyll's current status as a centre of seafood excellence.

Today's visitor to the West Coast is in for a culinary treat. From Oban to Campbeltown, Tighnabruaich to Tarbert, establishment owners, cooks and chefs are getting hold of the freshest of raw produce (by which we mean, quite literally, from the seawater to the plate) to create delicious menus that challenge anything a city centre has to offer. The ultimate in 'fast food' – lobster, langoustine, crab, halibut, oysters – all are to be found in abundance, served with flair and imagination by people committed to showcasing Argyll's seafood and shellfish.

The Seafood Trail meanders through some of the most spectacular scenery Scotland has to offer, enabling seafood junkies to sample, share and enjoy seafood and shellfish from a wide variety of establishments. From the freshest of crab rolls served with a squeeze of lemon and some home-made mayonnaise, to Michelin-rated menus that feature a wide range of beautifully prepared dishes, visitors to the trail are assured a warm welcome and an eating experience that values freshness and flair above all else.

What makes The Seafood Trail so refreshingly alive is the people who have created it. United by a common vision of showcasing the best of local produce simply because it is so good, many have taken huge risks to establish a standard of seafood cuisine that others might consider 'unnecessary' for such a rural part of Scotland. All of them believe that a crucial part of any holiday experience is the atmosphere surrounding the food that we eat on our travels. Building strong relationships with local suppliers is the underlying ethos of all those involved – no-one is in any doubt that the real heroes of The Seafood Trail are the fishermen who deliver the raw produce to the door.

Seafood Trail members have to meet exacting criteria and standards to be involved, and they're uniquely proud of the part their establishments have to play in welcoming visitors to a most beautiful part of Scotland.

The recipes included in this book veer towards the simple, partly because there is nothing unduly complicated about preparing a seafood meal, and partly because the natural flavours of seafood and shellfish are so wonderful that they require only the minimum of additional ingredients.

Food is but a part of the total, however, and in order to get a true feel for The Seafood Trail, you need to get to know the people behind it. Each has a unique story to share about their own journey to the West Coast of Scotland, and it is the overall 'personality' of each of the member establishments that makes a visit to the Seafood Trail so enjoyable.

From Crab Shack to Oyster Bar reveals a mouth-watering collection of seafood recipes from the owners, chefs and cooks who live and work here. Interspersed with local stories and background to the personalities behind the establishments, the featured recipes reflect a growing trend towards simplicity, both in terms of style and presentation.

The Seafood Trail is more than a journey. It's a sensory feast.

1 Seafood Cabin
2 The Anchor Hotel
3 The Hunting Lodge Hotel
4 The Tayvallich Inn
5 Dunvalanree House
6 Ee'usk
7 Cairnbaan Hotel
8 Laroch Foods
9 The Royal at Tighnabruaich
10 The Loch Fyne Oyster Bar

THE SEAFOOD CABIN

or 'crab shack' to the locals

Skipness Estate, Tarbert, Argyll, PA29 6XU

T: +44 (0)1880 760207
E: james@skipness.freeserve.co.uk
F: +44 (0)1880 760208
W: in progress

Season: From the Bank Holiday weekend at end of May until end of September. Open Sunday to Friday from 11am-6pm. Closed on Saturday. Directions: 12 miles (19km) south of Tarbert at the end of the B8001, off the A83.

It's not a route for the short days of winter; most reasonable creatures on the evolutionary upside of an oyster would probably choose to be curled up by the fireside. But for those hardy enough to make the journey 'cross-peninsula', they are rewarded with a vast stretch of open water, the Isle of Arran pencilled onto the horizon and an impressively craggy foreshore that is testament to the ruggedness of this natural, beautiful coastline.

Driving along the single-track road towards Skipness is an adventure. During the milder summer months, on the waterside, driftwood sculptures appear from nowhere. The odd camper van settles for the season, its solitary occupant happy to 'connect with the landscape' for a while at least. Remnants of a rock barbeque lie exposed to the elements and sheep stray onto the open road, claiming their heritable right to roam. No great hurry. No worry.

The village of Skipness is not quite the end of the road, but nearly; a mile further on, and slightly inland, the jagged outline of Skipness castle – a late 13th-century stronghold of the MacDonald clan – tempts visitors to explore still further. As you round a bend that brings the shore into view again, the Seafood Cabin sits in the middle of a kind of garden, kind of menagerie. Wooden benches and picnic tables provide somewhere to sit and watch. And there is much to see.

Fondly known as the 'crab shack' by those local to the area, the cabin was moved from Tarbert Pier in 1990. Boasting neither grand design nor particularly good looks ('still standing' would be a fair description) it is, however, uniquely fit for its purpose and frequently attracts returning visitors from home and overseas during its short summer season. The kind of place that you almost don't want anyone else to discover for fear of spoiling its character, the Seafood Cabin serves freshly-caught seafood and shellfish, a selection of home-baking and just the right combination of liquid refreshment with which to wash the whole lot down.

It's surprisingly difficult to organise an interview with owner Sophie James. Unlike other establishment owners included in this book, Sophie would appear to be even busier during the winter months than in summer. The Seafood Cabin rests within, and is part of, Skipness Castle estate, a working farm with way-marked walks through pastures, glens and woodland. Sophie's family have owned the estate since 1936, when her grandfather fell in love with the area and decided to retire there. He died in 1969 in a fire which claimed much of the family home which was subsequently rebuilt by estate workers.

Sophie took over the management of the estate when her grandmother was seriously ill. Hands-on, enthusiastic and a great lover of the practical outdoor life, she soon became farmer to 50 cows, 1000 sheep, a wide variety of domestic fowls, and the usual collection of

strays that tend to find their way to a friendly home. Winter/spring, as a consequence, is the time when neglected book-work is brought up to date, cattle are moved, sheep are lambed, holiday cottages (Sophie owns five in Skipness) are spring-cleaned and the extensive grounds are put to bed for the winter. All of which, not surprisingly, leaves little time for interviews.

Yet it is the enchanting haphazardness of clucking chickens sitting under your wooden bench table to catch the crumbs; of sheep wandering across the horizon; of umbrellas at the ready should the sky decide to dump its waterlogged contents on you for an hour or so, that make the unassuming Seafood Cabin so relentlessly popular. As much an experience for children as it is for the more discerning adult epicurean, Sophie is determined that her own good fortune at living where she does should be shared with as many people as possible. 'The estate is both a commitment and a responsibility,' she believes, 'and I love to see the children wander freely through the fields towards the sandy beach, or their parents exploring the chapel graveyard. Much of my time during the summer months is spent explaining our own, very short, food chain – people want to get closer to the producers and children are fascinated by all the gory details!' she says.

Horrified by the proliferation of 'private' signs that populate so much of Scotland's landscape, she is keen to 'de-sanitise' the countryside. 'Here in Skipness, we're not precious about sharing,' she says. 'So what if there are cows in the field? People should be able to walk; to get places; to enjoy what many others simply take for granted.'

The family home itself doubles as a wonderfully comfortable guest house, with three bed and breakfast rooms and a guest dining room which boasts views, from three sides, across Kilbrannan Sound, Skipness Castle and the chapel graveyard. The furniture is huge, squashy and lived-in. Family portrait photos, stuffed animals and local landscapes adorn walls and surfaces. Dogs bark at your feet in the hallway. Books and magazines invite you to learn more about the history of a place that has seen many changes both in the recent and distant past.

Sophie's mother, Libby, an elderly lady who looks as equally hands-on, but a tad more weather-beaten than her daughter, helps with the food preparation for the cabin during the summer, endlessly dressing the crabs delivered to her door by the local Skipness fishermen. 'You need to handle crab immediately,' she says. 'They don't benefit from hanging around so we often sit into the small hours "crabbing".'

Home-grown produce features heavily – a wide variety of lettuce, tomatoes, peppers, herbs and cucumbers are harvested in abundance in season and served with shellfish. The infamous orange cake – popular with young and old alike – boasts duck eggs for its lightness and rich colouring. Smoked products – trout and salmon primarily – come from her brother's smokery on Arran. 'We nip across on the ferry from Claonaig and pick up whatever we need   Arran to us is as local as Tarbert on the other side of Kintyre.'

Neither of them work to particular recipes, referring instead to 'handfuls of whatever herbs happen to be in season,' and 'jam-jar quantities', and 'a splash of this, and a splash of that.' Scribbled menus, handed down through the family, play a big part. With no tricks to hide behind, the recipes that follow are, consequently, somewhat haphazard – measurements are a guide rather than a given and ingredients as much a matter of taste as is their seasonality.

Sophie is bemused at the idea of being featured in a cookery book: She doesn't believe herself to 'share the same chef-space' as others featured and is modest about the food that she does serve. This is undoubtedly part of the charm of a place that makes few grand claims yet delivers some of the genuinely simpler pleasures in life.

Whole salmon, 'Aga-baked' in wet newspaper

Ideally you need an Aga for this – if you bake this in a conventional oven it's a bit like using a gas barbeque instead of a charcoal one. If you have an electric fan oven with a slow-cook setting, use that instead.

Ingredients

1 whole salmon – gutted and cleaned
1 newspaper – ideally the *Oban Times* according to Sophie's mother with any colour newsprint removed!
2 lemons – quartered
Wild garlic
Fresh dill

Method

Steep the whole newspaper in cold tap water and squeeze out any excess. Place the whole salmon in the centre of the opened newspaper and stuff it with the lemon quarters, wild garlic and dill. Wrap tightly and place on a large baking tray that you know will fit in your Aga or fan oven.

Cook in the low oven of your Aga (or on the slow-cook setting of your fan oven) for between 1-2 hours, depending on the size of the salmon. To check if the fish is cooked, pierce with a sharp skewer through the newspaper and the salmon; if the skewer comes out clean, the salmon is ready.

When ready, unwrap the fish and serve direct from the newspaper (a great conversation piece!). Let your guests help themselves and serve with rocket and dandelion leaf salad and a warm potato salad.

Shell-on langoustine served with Sophie's fresh herb dip

Langoustines are large prawns – sometimes referred to as Dublin Bay prawns or Norway lobsters. They are plentiful in Scotland's West Coast waters and require only the minimum of cooking and handling.
Wild garlic grows in damp, shaded and boggy conditions. Sophie picks the long green leaves fresh from the bottom of her drive and uses it both as a garnish (it has lovely white flowers in the spring) and as a flavouring in butters and in stock. It's also excellent thrown onto hot barbeque coals.

Ingredients
6 langoustines per person
⅓ jam jar natural yoghurt
⅔ jam jar good quality mayonnaise
A handful of wild garlic leaves, finely chopped
Fresh dill – chopped
Lemon thyme – chopped
Flat leaf parsley – chopped
Chervil – chopped

Method
Plunge the langoustines into water that has just boiled and has been turned down to simmering point for 30-40 seconds: no more. Remove the langoustines and leave to cool naturally.

Remove the gut (sometimes referred to as the 'black line' from the langoustines by taking the middle segment of the tail shell between thumb and forefinger then twisting it and pulling gently. This should remove the entire gut entrail in one go. If it doesn't, don't worry – it can be removed after they are served.

Combine the remaining ingredients in a bowl, stir until well mixed. Serve the cooled langoustines with the fresh herb dip.

Orange cake

A combination of the duck egg yolks and the orange concentrate gives this cake a lovely rich colour.

Ingredients

3 duck eggs
6 oz/175g flour
6 oz/175g caster sugar
6 oz/175g margarine
Orange concentrate
2 x 8-in/20-cm sandwich tins lined with greaseproof paper and pre-greased

For the filling

4 tbs/60ml boiling water
6 oz/175g butter or soft margarine
9-12 oz/250-350g icing sugar, sifted
2 drops vanilla essence

Method

Cream the margarine and sugar together. Add the duck eggs one at a time, along with 1 tbs of flour to each egg. Fold in the remaining flour and a dash of orange concentrate.

Divide the sponge mixture between the two sandwich tins and bake in the top Aga oven (or at 325°F/160°C) for about 20 minutes. Check that the sponges are cooked by piercing them with a skewer in the centre. If the sponges are ready, the skewer will come out clean. Allow to cool and remove from sandwich tins.

To finish

After the sponges are cool, spread the filling ingredients evenly on the top of one of the sponges and place the other on top of this.

The Anchor Hotel

Harbour Street, Tarbert, Argyll, PA29 6UB

T: +44 (0)1880 820577
E: anchorhotel@lochfyne-scotland.co.uk
F: +44 (0)1880 820577
W: www.lochfyne-scotland.co.uk

'we do nothing with the majority of ingredients except cook them and sometimes we don't even do that'

Children mistake it for Archie's Castle in *Balamory* and holiday-making parents, too wearied to argue, cross their fingers behind their backs and tell their excitable off-spring that it probably is. Which it isn't, of course. Wrong pink. Wrong location.

The Anchor Hotel is very pink. A subtler shade admittedly, since I toned down the original fuschia hue with something a little more tasteful. But pink nonetheless, a welcoming beacon for yachtsmen bringing their boats to berth in one of the prettiest natural harbours in Scotland.

Sandwiched between a surprisingly smart boutique on the one side and the 'Austrian-looking Scottish' bar next door, the Anchor clashes humorously with its surroundings. More of a dining pub with rooms than a hotel, the cosy candlelit bar overlooks the harbour. At low tide, herons balance proudly on rock beds and boats rest, tummy down, on the mud. When the tide comes in, fishing boats berth against the harbour wall, offloading their catch on the quayside. You can literally watch your dinner being landed whilst enjoying a pint of the local ale or a glass of wine.

My daughter describes life here as 'living on a post-

card', and every day as I stroll down to the hotel I'm struck by the absolute beauty of where we are. As a family we moved to Tarbert more by chance than design. Having sailed and holidayed frequently in the area, I was interviewing the previous owner of The Anchor for an article that I was writing and on hearing that the hotel was for sale, I negotiated its purchase and moved to the area a week before Tarbert's infamous Music Festival.

To be recommended? I'm wary of overselling the dream. Our first six months were difficult. The timing of my entry to the world as a hotelier was not quite the gentle 'easing in' that I'd envisaged – and if I'm honest, I didn't really have a clue what I was doing. I'd never worked behind a bar, for instance, in my life, and I think that it was probably a combination of complete naivety, a good bar manager and genuinely friendly customers which kept me going.

Working almost without sleep for the first three weeks, I found the hotel business initially physically and mentally exhausting. I threw myself completely into the challenge and did everything that everyone else should have been doing simply so that I knew how the whole thing worked. Somewhat ironic, then, that in a move intended to pull the family together, I saw less of my children than in my previous life when commuting to Glasgow.

Overall, however, the move has been a positive one, and moulding the hotel to suit my own vision for it has been an enjoyable challenge. Being so familiar with the area, I had a very clear idea of what was needed. Comfortable rooms that overlooked the water; furnishings that reflected the coastal location but never competed with it; books and magazines that visitors could browse whilst watching the world go by from the bar; paintings and artefacts that give a real sense of 'place'. Nothing complicated. 'Simple comfort' is how I describe the overall atmosphere of The Anchor.

Re-working the menu has been the greatest challenge. I inherited a menu that, to my mind, didn't really exploit the abundance of natural produce that Loch Fyne has to offer. I don't enjoy heavily spiced and flavoured foods and am of the opinion that 'less is more' when it comes to cooking with seafood and shellfish. Employing a good chef was critical and I 'tried and tested' a good few

Lemon Posset

This has to be one of the easiest, sexiest and most refreshing desserts ever and only takes minutes to make. The trick is to keep stirring! For an extra zing, add a teaspoon of good-quality lemon curd to each glass before pouring in the warmed posset mixture. Serve with your choice of blueberry compote; strawberry coulis; fresh berries and a dusting of icing sugar or with shortbread biscuits for dipping. Serves two.

Ingredients
284ml carton of double cream (9½ fl oz)
2¾ oz/75g caster sugar
2 medium lemons, juiced (but only after having 'zested' the skin, for garnish later)
2 sprigs of lemon thyme

Method
Pour the cream and sugar into a small saucepan. Slowly bring to the boil, stirring constantly to dissolve the sugar. Once it is boiling, cook for a further three minutes (precisely), still stirring constantly.

Remove from the heat and pour in half the lemon juice whilst stirring the mixture thoroughly. It should start to thicken instantly. Taste the mixture and if its not quite tart enough for your taste then put a little more juice in. It should be nice and tangy but still very rich.

Allow the posset to cool for approximately five minutes and then pour into two glasses. The posset will start to visibly thicken as it hits the cool glass. Cover with clingfilm and chill in the fridge for at least three hours. The posset should be quite firmly set when you come to serve it. Garnish with compote, if liked, and/or a sprig of lemon thyme and some zested lemon.

before finally finding someone whose own 'simple' cooking style reflected my own.

Consequently, the menu now displayed on the driftwood board outside favours what my chef Michael Staniland and I describe as 'pared-down' food. We do nothing with the majority of ingredients except cook them and sometimes we don't even do that. The most important thing, I believe, is to get the basics right. Our langoustines are cooked in boiling water – unsalted because the langoustines are as briny as the sea loch they come from. Then they are chilled under cold, running tap water so that the meat doesn't become mushy. We serve them piled high on a platter and leave the customer the pleasure of cracking, breaking and poking the shells. A dollop of home-made lemon mayonnaise on the side, a slice of freshly baked whole-grain bread – you really don't get faster, simpler food.

I also believe that while shellfish should be *cooked* simply, the *serving* of it should be full-on theatrical. We serve our seafood platters on huge, colourful dishes and as they're carried high to the table, the diners' reaction to how the platter looks is an essential part of their eating experience as a whole.

But this is a dining pub, remember. Diners are as likely to be seen getting 'tucked in' to a plate of breaded haddock and chips, served with a home-made tartare sauce, as they are to be found grappling crustaceans. Pretentiousness has no place at The Anchor table.

A large blackboard on the wall features the seafood specials, determined each day by whatever is landed on the quay. Puddings are proudly highlighted in red chalk: blueberry brûlé, lemon posset, bitter chocolate torte with crème fraîche, and a crumble of the day. Cheeses are all local – mostly from Arran and Mull, and the wine list is straightforward and reasonably priced. Sancerre, chablis, pinot grigio – sharp, clean-flavoured wines to complement a menu that is seafood led.

Different, but subtly so, is how I describe the gentle revamping of The Anchor. Longstanding customers, dressed casually in jeans and fleeces, can't quite put their finger on what's changed so feel comfortable returning to a place that has always been their friend. The chat's the same – sailing stories, or fishing ones, or golfing ones – and you're as likely to find a pair of sailing wellies at the entrance as you are walking boots, or diving gear or a bucket of herrings deposited by a passing Irish fisherman. Visit The Anchor on a busy Friday night during the summer and you'll find that the people enjoying the relaxed atmosphere inside reflect the activities, past-times and livelihoods that characterise this part of Argyll.

The Anchor Surf and Turf

This is a delicious and eye-catching mackerel, black pudding and haggis stack with burnished balsamic butter. Serves six.

Ingredients
12 mackerel fillets (Mine are caught by my son, Ben, most days – you might have to get yours from the local fishmongers. Look for firm shiny skin and a fish that isn't limp.)
6 slices of black pudding (preferably MacLeod's Stornoway black pudding)
6 slices of haggis
A dessert spoon of butter
Balsamic vinegar
1 lemon, cut into wedges
Butter, cut into small pieces to fleck the fish with before grilling

Method
Grill the slices of black pudding and haggis on both sides until just cooked and keep them warm in a low oven. Butter an oven tray and place the mackerel fillets skin-side-up on to the tray. Add the wedges of lemon and dot the mackerel skin with the flecks of butter.

Grill until the skin starts to bubble and reserve the lemon wedges.

Whilst you are grilling the mackerel, add the dessertspoon of butter to a small pan and heat quickly until brown. Add 2 teaspoonfuls of balsamic vinegar (take care at this point as the vinegar can catch fire, particularly if you're using a gas hob), and remove from the heat. Swirl the mixture in the pan until the vinegar and the butter are well combined. You will notice that the butter and vinegar splits. It's meant to. Add the residual lemony butter juices from the grilled mackerel.

Put one slice of black pudding on top of one piece of haggis per serving. Place the mackerel fillets on top and pour the balsamic butter over and around the stack.

Garnish with the grilled lemon.

Scallops grilled with Crabbies Green Ginger

This is simplicity itself and the grilled scallops are served with a green pea mash. Serves six.

Ingredients

30 scallops in their half shells, roes attached
Crabbies Green Ginger (don't use imitations)
A handful of rocket leaves
Ground Pepper
Well-creamed mashed potatoes (made with butter and cream)
Small bag of petit pois, cooked until soft
Lemon
Limes
Extra virgin olive oil
Black pepper

Method

Arrange the scallops in their half shells on three large baking trays. Pour over a generous splash of Crabbies and place under a hot grill until the scallops have just turned from opaque to white. (You may have to grill them in batches. Keep the ones that you have grilled warm in a low oven, or on top of the grill if it's an eye level type.) NB: Stand well back from the grill while the scallops are cooking – they have a tendency to spit!

Liquidise the cooked peas with the juice of the lemon when the scallops are being grilled. Add the mash to a liquidiser and zap the peas and the potatoes until well combined and a beautiful pea-green colour.

Put a spoonful of mash in the centre of each plate. Pile some rocket on top and drizzle with olive oil and a good grinding of black pepper. Arrange the scallops in their shells around the mash and serve with wedges of lemon and lime.

IOLAIR (Eagle) built circa 1900 and restored in 2005 in Tarbert

Clinker-built timber boats propelled by oar and wind have been used on the West Coast of Scotland for hundreds of years with boatbuilding methods and design showing a clear Norse influence. There are many variations but fishing boats were generally double-ended craft built of larch and oak with a lug sail and in later years a jib and bowsprit. In Loch Fyne small skiffs developed into larger boats up to some 37ft (11m) used for ring-netting at the end of the 19th century. These boats had a distinctive underwater shape and steeply raked stern post. This became known as 'The Loch Fyne Skiff'.

Many of these craft were built in Tarbert and Ardrishaig but *IOLAIR* was built in Port Bannatyne on Bute. One hundred years ago the harbour in Tarbert would be full of similar craft.

The larger Skiffs were used for ring-net herring fishing but smaller craft like *IOLAIR* would be used for line fishing and pot laying. Originally skiffs would be propelled by wind and oars alone but many were later fitted with engines like *IOLAIR*. The design of the stern meant that the engines were fitted off centre with the propeller on one side of the hull. Nets would normally be cast on the opposite side to avoid fouling.

IOLAIR is fully functioning and is sailed at village festivals and local yacht club events.

Robert McPhail

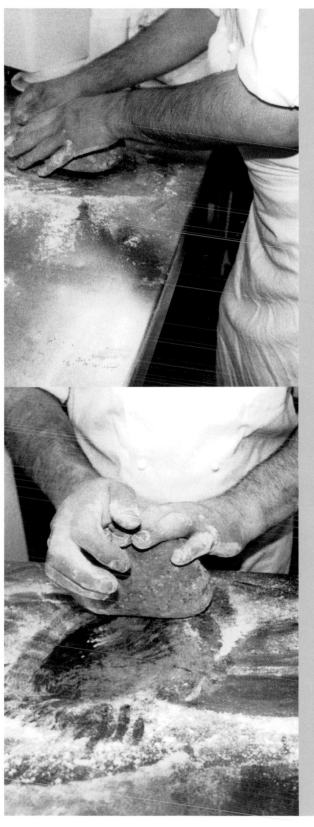

The Anchor Soda Bread

We make about a dozen soda loaves a day, sometimes more, and use it to accompany soups, to soak up the juices from mussels and scallops and as an accompaniment (toasted) to our house pâté and crab salad. If we have any left over the next day (which isn't often), we serve it toasted at breakfast time.

Ingredients

2 tbs/30ml dark treacle
10 fl oz/300ml milk (approximately) or add 2 oz unsalted butter, melted, to 10 fl oz of ordinary milk
1½ tbs sugar
4½ oz wholemeal flour
3 oz/75g porridge oats
½ tsp salt
1 tsp cream of tartar
1 tsp bicarbonate of soda
Good pinch of ground ginger

Method

Heat the treacle and milk/butter together. Mix all the dry ingredients together: Add the treacle and milk mixture until a soft dough is achieved. With floured hands, shape into a round cake about 1½ in/40mm thick. Using a bread knife, make a large cross on the top of the cake.

Place on a floured baking sheet and bake at 400°F/200°C for 40 minutes.

The Hunting Lodge Hotel

Bellochantuy, Kintyre, Argyll, PA28 6QR

T: +44 (0)1583 421323
E: email@thehuntinglodgehotel.com
F: +44 (0)1583 421343
W: www.thehuntinglodgehotel.com

'I'm a simple farmer with a fond liking for a small libation'

Intriguingly contrary is perhaps the simplest way to describe the Duke of Argyll's former Hunting Lodge at Bellochantuy. Built in 1872, the recently extended exterior belies the history that has been carefully preserved within. Palm trees populate the grounds that hug Kintyre's Atlantic coast; the distant islands of Islay, Jura and Ireland appear sometimes moody, sometimes romantic, sometimes not at all on the far horizon. From the private beach in front of the hotel visitors can watch the afternoon dissolve into a rosy dusk one day, only to witness surfers braving the Atlantic rollers the next. Wild weather is as integral to this coast of Kintyre as the gannets, the shell-strewn sands and the pods of porpoises frolicking only a short way offshore.

Owners Stuairdh and Libby Hammond are contrary too: what little of Stuairdh's face isn't covered in beard bears the hallmarks of someone who has spent much of his life outdoors, and remarkably little of it in Scotland. A pioneer in his youth, he moved from a large-scale dairy farm in Norfolk in the late 1970's to Tristán da Cuña – the most remote inhabited island in the world – simply because he felt like a change! There he farmed mainly sheep and cattle and also took up posts as conservation officer and accounts officer for the local government office.

He arrived on the island with three children, left with four and spent the next ten years as an advisor to various governments in Morocco, Portugal, the then Czechoslovakia and Poland. At various other times he ran a tissue culture laboratory multiplying plants by cloning and helped to privatise dairy state farms in Poland. 'There's very little difference between cows and customers,' he now contests, drawing comparison with his life as an hotelier. 'The nicer you treat them both, the better you feed them, and the more attention you pay to the simplest of their needs, the happier the outcome.'

Stuairdh is, in truth, beyond contrary. Eccentric perhaps better defines a man who sports a kilt in all weathers, pops across to Poland as regularly as most of us might visit the local supermarket and insists on sharing his love of Campbeltown malt whisky with many an unsuspecting visitor. 'I'm a simple farmer,' he says, 'with a fond liking for a small libation.' His welcoming manner is also blunt – don't veer into political discussion without first sharpening your verbal armoury, and don't, whatever you do, mention the fact that so much of the West Coast of Scotland's seafood and shellfish ends up being consumed in Spain.

This is a particularly mute point, not least because Stuairdh's own experience suggests a strong local and visiting market for seafood sourced in local Kintyre waters. It is a fact that nearly 90% of all local catch goes overseas, 'because the demand for shellfish in particular is so strong,' he says. Whilst acknowledging that fishermen have an absolute right to earn their living however they choose, he decries the supermarket chains that drive down the price of Scottish-caught produce, effectively 'devaluing the producers whilst driving up the cost of seafood and shellfish to the local market.'

'Your average consumer is denied access to the wide range of products caught in local Scottish waters because creating an environment of scarcity undoubtedly pushes prices up,' Stuairdh believes. 'More and more

Baked cod with Arran mustard on a red wine sauce

This is a fantastically meaty fish dish – the red wine and beef stock sauce is a hearty, cold-weather combination and you need to choose a well-rounded red wine to maximise both the flavour and the colour. Serves four.

Ingredients

4 chunky pieces of cod fillet
(approximately 7 oz/200g each)
3 oz/75g melted butter
2 dessert spoons of whole-grain Arran mustard
10 fl oz/300ml good beef stock
10 fl oz/300ml well-rounded red wine (Merlot is good for the colour)
Salt and pepper to season
Freshly cut dill

Method

Pour the beef stock and red wine into a thick-based pan and boil until reduced by half. Meanwhile, place the fillets of cod on an oven-proof tray. Pour the melted butter over the fish and place them in a hot oven (400°F/200°C) for approximately 10 minutes. When cooked, remove the cod from the oven, coat the fillets lightly with the whole-grain Arran mustard and return them to the oven for a further two minutes – no more!

Pour the red wine sauce onto four warm plates. Place the cod fillets on top and garnish them with some dill. Serve with baby potatoes and a mixed leaf salad.

fishmongers are closing down, partly because regulations are so onerous (do not get him started on regulations!) and partly because consumers are unfamiliar with the wide range of seafood and shellfish available.'

Stuairdh has worked hard to build a strong relationship with his own local suppliers and is pleased that more and more hoteliers are doing the same, primarily because building a strong local market 'proves to our local fisherman that we, at least, value what they do'. Interestingly, therefore, he is happy to pay more per langoustine than his Spanish counterparts. 'Being able to

sell in volume overseas on the one hand enables our fishermen to sell on a smaller scale locally,' he argues, 'and anyway, our customers are happy to pay a fair price in our own restaurant and bar for a menu that is so abundantly fresh.'

The Hunting Lodge's menu benefits from a confidently unshowy chef who cooks in a manner that perfectly reflects the location. Visually unrefined in presentation, a generous chunk of cod in a wholegrain Arran mustard gravy would gratify the strictest of carnivores; thick and as flavoursome as a piece of prime Scotch fillet. It is

Grilled sardines with spinach and tomato salsa

This is simplicity itself and is delicious fast food. The quantities below will serve four as a starter.

Ingredients

4 fresh sardines (3-4 oz/80-100g each)
9 oz/260g fresh spinach
2 oz/50g butter
Olive oil
Grated nutmeg
Black Pepper
Sea Salt
Fresh rosemary

For the tomato salsa

4 plum tomatoes, skinned, de-seeded and diced
2 red onions, finely diced
2 tbs/30ml virgin olive oil
Handful of freshly chopped basil

Peel the plum tomatoes by scoring the skins in four quarters with a sharp knife and steeping them in boiled water for two minutes. Remove them from the water with a draining spoon and allow them to cool. The skins can then be easily removed. Remove the

seeds from the tomatoes and chop the remaining flesh. Mix all the salsa ingredients together and let them stand for at least 10 minutes before serving with the sardines.

Method

Put the butter and olive oil in a pan and heat gently. Add the spinach and toss until the butter melts and the leaves wilt. Add a little grated nutmeg and black pepper.

Gut and clean the sardines. Cut three scores on each side of the fish. Fill the cavity with the buttered spinach and lay the sardines on a lightly greased baking tray.

Brush the fish sparsely with olive oil and season with ground sea salt and black pepper. Add some generous sprigs of rosemary. Place the stuffed sardines under a hot grill and turn them when the top side is cooked; this takes approximately five minutes. Grill the other side, this time only for three minutes.

Place the fish on top of dressed mixed leaves and serve with a fresh tomato salsa.

Salmon with a fresh herb crust and velvety Pernod sauce

Pernod and seafood is a tantalising combination; the aniseed flavour suiting, in particular, salmon and trout. Serves four.

Ingredients

4 salmon fillet steaks (6-7 oz/175 200g each)
3 oz/75g melted butter
Fresh white bread crumbs
Flat leaf parsley, chopped
Fresh tarragon, chopped
Zest of one lime
Sea Salt
Black pepper
Fennel, to garnish

For the Pernod sauce

2 oz/50g butter
4 oz/100g leeks, finely sliced
1 fl oz/25ml Pernod
10 fl oz/300ml double cream
Seasoning

Lightly sauté the finely sliced leeks in the butter. Pour in the Pernod slowly and burn off the alcohol. This is easier to do on a gas hob when all you need to do is tilt the pan towards the flame; otherwise you will have to ignite the vapour. Remember to stand well back. Add the double cream, stir and bring to the boil. Simmer until the sauce begins to thicken. Season to taste.

Method

Mix the breadcrumbs, herbs, lime zest and the seasoning together. Place the salmon fillets on an oven-proof dish. Pour half of the melted butter over the salmon and top each fillet with the crust mix.

Now pour the remaining melted butter over the salmon and place in a medium hot oven (350°F/175°C) for approximately 5-10 minutes until the salmon is still firm and just cooked.

Spoon some of the Pernod sauce on to the middle of a dinner plate. Place the salmon on top, garnish with fennel and serve with buttered new potatoes.

complemented, strangely, (but like everything else in this contrary setting, it works) by a rich, red wine sauce laced with nutty mustard. The fillet of seabass is better than the jet set could ever find in Antibes, considerably cheaper and most likely fresher to boot.

In the autumn, locally landed herring and mackerel are served simply – the former in oatmeal perhaps, the latter grilled with peppered lemon butter, or soused in white wine vinegar, vine tomato and home-grown dill: comforting, familiar food.

Wife Libby Kerr-Hammond, the quieter of the two, more cautious, less vocal and forever patient with a husband whose predilection for local malt undoubtedly leaves her 'resolutely uninspired at times', none-the-less plays an integral role in the overall ambience that is The Hunting Lodge. She's the soother, calming the odd heated moment; the clear thinker, applying common sense to some of Stuairdh's more 'off the wall' episodes; the nurturer, ensuring hard working staff are well fed and well rested. She's also a keen gardener, responsible for the increasingly productive herb garden. First and foremost she is a mother – happy to welcome her children home from successful careers further afield.

The homely interior is undoubtedly down to Libby – a huge roaring log fire provides the perfect setting for an end of meal coffee – or if Stuairdh gets his way, something significantly stronger. The glass-fronted porch that runs the width of the building boasts comfy sofas, books of local interest and a telescope that lets you study a pair of otters or a pod of porpoise without getting either too close, or too wet.

Outside, in the height of stormy winter, the large rock formations that edge the private beach shelter the lodge from the worst of the wind and the weather that the Atlantic Ocean can sometimes hurl in its direction. But in the unique way that is The Hunting Lodge, you might also find yourself facing the winter sun, supping wine on the sheltered patio and wondering whether your next move should be a barefoot stroll, a short round of crazy golf or a less energetic study of a menu designed to truly feed the soul.

The Tayvallich Inn

Tayvallich, By Lochgilphead, Argyll, PA31 8PL

T: +44 (0)1546 870282
E: roddy.anderson@tayvallich-inn.com
F: +44(0)1546 870333
W: www.tayvallich-inn.com

'Tayvallich's greatest charm is that nothing much happens here'

Immediately after lunch is served during the mild summer months at the Tayvallich Inn, customers often witness the chef running out of the kitchen, his wet-suit half-hoisted, to the beach frontage that lies on the other side of Tayvallich's single road. Stopping only momentarily to build the flatpack that is his single-handed trapeze Contender dinghy, Roddy Anderson then goes sailing until it's time to start cooking again. A little bizarre perhaps, but then he is a very relaxed cook.

In the quieter winter months, when the weather is less clement and the local waters a degree or three less inviting, Roddy prefers to sail in warmer climes and on bigger boats. Last winter, he delivered a yacht across the Atlantic to the British Virgin Isles. In years past he was a professional yachtsman and ski instructor. He's visited 40 countries and was once chased by pirates in the Red Sea.

He also happens to own the local bus company – an incidental snippet of information that is actually quite significant because Roddy bought the bus company from his father, Fergie Anderson who operated Anderson coaches from a garage at the head of the bay. This was then converted into what is now the Tayvallich Inn in 1976. He then sold the Inn to John Grafton who, over an 18-year period built up a sizeable reputation for steak and seafood. So when Roddy took over the thorny crown of succession and bought the Inn back from more recent owners in 2001, he was actually reclaiming a little bit of family history.

A wanderer at heart, Roddy the chef and respectable establishment owner had come home to develop a style of cooking which, if you were to describe it by the origins of the ingredients, would be 'Scottish with strong Mediterranean influences'.

And to this day, the floor in the bar still slopes gently towards the window where they used to roll the buses out.

Roddy is a big personality. He talks to everyone and anyone when behind the bar, which happens to be the only one in the picturesque fishing village that boasts a resident population of less than 100. His local customers are a diverse cross section of people: some have moved to the area to escape previous city lives and are now able to run relatively large businesses from home thanks to good internet access. Others have been drawn to the area because their children can live the cliché of wandering safely and being 'well looked out for'. It's also a natural draw for artists – John Lowrie Morrison is a near native now – and for sailors enjoying the sheltered waters at the top of Loch Sween.

His entry in to the world of cooking was, Roddy admits, a baptism of fire. Budgeting and costing came naturally to him; on one of the large boats he skippered he had a £750k budget. However, getting the kitchen and the menu running to his taste was more of a challenge and consequently his first season was, undoubtedly, his hardest.

For a start, the menu hadn't changed in nearly eight years. He had also inherited chefs who were unhappy with Roddy's vision for what was now, after all, his establishment. On 21 June 2002 – a date embalmed in Roddy's memory banks – a complement of chefs walked

Loch Fyne Oysters pan fried in butter with chervil and cream

This recipe is perfect for anyone who prefers their oysters cooked, even though it is the flavour of the oysters that lingers the longest.

Ingredients

6 oysters per person
1 wedge of butter
1 glass of white wine
Handful of chervil, chopped
Small carton of double cream
Gruyère cheese

Method

Take 6 oysters per person. Shuck them carefully by inserting an oyster knife between the shell halves, and by twisting the blade, gently separate them. Reserve the oyster juice and place the oysters in a large frying pan and fry them gently in the butter. Remove the oysters and keep warm.

Add the oyster juice to the butter left in the pan and reduce this until almost evaporated. Add a glass of good dry white wine and reduce again. Add half the chopped chervil and enough cream to make a pouring sauce. Place the oysters back into the cream sauce, add the remainder of the chervil and stir.

Put the oysters back in their shells on a baking tray, pour any sauce left in the pan over them equally and then top with Gruyère and glaze under a hot grill.

out leaving Roddy to man a kitchen that was finally, and ironically, his own.

Surprised at how much technique he had absorbed from the now absent chefs, this sudden role shift afforded Roddy the opportunity to create the kind of menu with which he was most comfortable. Simple food that combined the best of local produce with his favourite Mediterranean herbs and spices: chargrilled whole bream with beurre blanc and fennel; cold lobster (brought in fresh from the outer rafts by boat every morning) served in the half shell with tropical fruit salad; Loch Fyne oysters; scallops and black pudding. He loves fennel, tarragon, chervil, rosemary and basil, and accompanying vegetable dishes and salads owe much of their flavour to these herbs.

Whilst the food has undergone somewhat radical remodelling, such revolutionary chic has not been applied to the interior, which to the delight of customers has changed remarkably little over the last few years. A crammed notice board indicates a real village local whilst still providing the kind of useful information that makes visitors feel at home. Both the informal bar area and the restaurant housed in the conservatory overlook the sheltered Loch a'Bhealaich with its scattering of yachts moored informally around the bay; and whilst the restaurant is unpretentiously 'smarter', one menu applies throughout and dress code is resolutely relaxed.

Paintings by John Lowrie Morrison (better known as JoLoMo) add a strong splash of colour to otherwise light walls. In the winter, when the days are short and the sun sits low in the sky, iron stoves throw a welcoming warmth in the direction of customers fresh from the hills or a gentle hike from the neighbouring hamlet of Carsaig, a tiny settlement wrapped around a shingle bay.

Tayvallich's greatest charm is that nothing much happens here, affording anyone passing by the chance to simply be. You can only approach the village in a leisurely way, either by boat or winding single-track road. Fashion and trends remain remarkably overlooked and whilst the rest of life marches apace, often it is only the sound of gulls that fills the space between sea and sky.

Roddy's enthusiasm for the life he leads is probably the most energy expended by anyone falling victim to Tayvallich's sleepy charm. Visitors return home determined to give up their own rat race in the not too distant future, heartened by a cook who sails between courses and leads the kind of spirited life to which so many aspire.

Crab, apple and fennel salad

The perfect light lunch. Good fishmongers now have fresh crab meat readily available. White meat is best but add some brown as well if you want to.

Ingredients

Fresh picked white crab meat
½ a fresh fennel bulb, sliced thinly
1 fresh red chilli, seeds removed and finely chopped
1 eating apple, chopped
Juice of 1 lemon
Juice of 1 lime
1 chopped shallot
1 tbs/15ml of soured cream
Small bunch of rocket
4 sliced new potatoes (cooked)
Chilli oil (optional)

Method

Slice the new potatoes and put in a mixing bowl with the rest of the ingredients and mix together. Place a generous helping into each bowl and dress with a little chilli oil if desired.

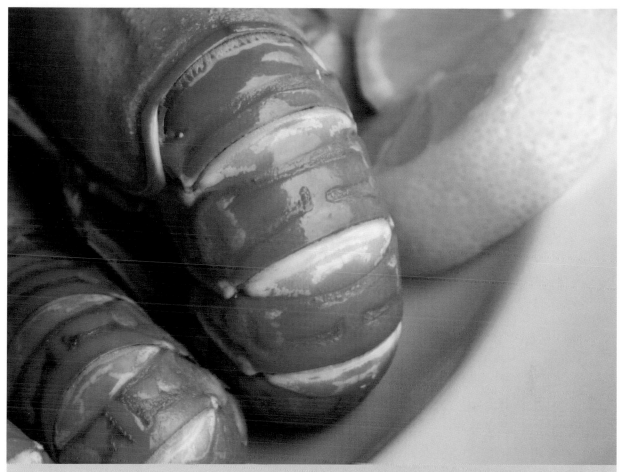

Loch Sween prawns with a tarragon and Pernod dressing

If you can't get live prawns for this dish, make sure the ones that you do use are really fresh.

Ingredients

6 large live prawns per serving
Chopped tarragon, flat leaf parsley and chervil
Soy sauce
Honey
Olive oil
Pernod
Lemon juice

Method

For large prawns, blanch in boiling water for about four minutes. Allow them to cool slightly, then using a large sharp cook's knife, split the prawns each in half, lengthways.

For the dressing, add a splash of soy and Pernod into a bowl, then add a teaspoon of honey and some olive oil, then some lemon juice and herbs. Warm the dressing gently in a small pan – it should be only baby-bath warm.

Arrange the warm split prawns randomly on a warm plate, and spoon over the dressing. Serve with a wedge of lemon.

Dunvalanree House

Port Righ Bay by Carradale, Kintyre, Argyll PA28 6SE

T: +44 (0)1583 431226
E: bookin@dunvalanree.com
F: +44 (0)1583 431339
W: www.dunvalanree.com

'Alyson is a cook who loves to cook'

Paul McCartney's 'Long and Winding Road' was, apparently, inspired by the stretch of single-track road that lines the East Kintyre coast from Clanoaig to Carradale. Climbing steeply in parts, the intrepid driver can look down on Arran's familiar contours before rolling leisurely down to the picturesque Carradale Glen and the tiny hamlet of Grogport – a higgledy piggledy collection of seaside cottages that nestle, colour-coded, side by side.

A few miles further on, Carradale is signposted sharp left. A mile beyond that, a narrow road to the right delivers you, after the odd wind and turn, to Dunvalanree, an impressive looking house perched on a cliff on Port Righ Bay – the tiny sheltered enclave where Robert the Bruce landed in 1306. Nowadays the bay would more likely be the idyllic setting for a children's adventure film or an Agatha Christie novel.

Bought 'on a whim' in 1999 by Alan and Alyson Milstead, the four-star small hotel provides both real home comforts and an absolute sense of 'place' to visitors from around the world. Dunvalanree feels 'lived in': hints of a growing family are evident in the photographs and books that litter surfaces, and the son and daughter still living at home are responsible for much of the outdoor clothing and paraphernalia that hangs from a multitude of laden hooks in the downstairs cloakroom. If you want a sense of the lives that families actually lead in such beautiful, middle-of-nowhere settings, a visit to Dunvalanree will provide precisely that.

Each of the five carefully decorated en-suite bedrooms boast stunning views towards either the bay or Kilbrannan Sound, and the expanse of windows in both the impressive guest lounge and the dining room frame an ever-changing seascape and a cliff garden that survives, somehow, from year to year. Coal fires, piled high with logs and driftwood collected from the shore, tempt you to stay indoors to while away the time. Outside the dolphins, whales and otters that come into view (dependent on weather and season) remind you that this sheltered cove is a true nature lover's paradise and that perhaps you'd better get your wellies on and head outdoors.

Alyson is the cook – self-taught, not particularly comfortable talking about herself and to be found, most often, preparing various menus in the small kitchen that leads directly onto the dining room. She admits that whilst neither of them is a fan of fads or culinary revolutions, she is a bit of a jackdaw, picking up snippets and ideas from many of the hotels and restaurants she enjoys visiting during the quieter winter months. Not surprisingly, therefore, her style and menu has changed significantly over the last few years, and guests enjoying a table d'hôte menu these days are quick to acknowledge her as an extraordinarily gifted cook.

She's also a brave cook; happy to experiment with different flavours, colours, textures and methods that include pairing seared scallops and cherry tomatoes with a pastel-coloured basil ice cream. Or how about smoking chicken in a covered wok with tea, rice and honey to produce a wonderful basis for a spring salad? In Alyson's hands, ingredients take on a particular delicacy – she has a talent, somehow, for making scallops, or cod, or sole taste more of itself than the original ingredient.

The basics don't escape a close attention to detail,

either: soups are subtly spiced – cumin with lentil, coriander with carrot; and salads are lightly and subtly dressed. Her home-made breads are served at breakfast and dinner and their slow-baking twice a day diffuses, throughout the hotel, the kind of aroma that encourages you not to wander too far in case your tastebuds miss out on something truly wonderful. Alyson is a cook who loves to cook.

Happier front stage (not least because the kitchen is most definitely his wife's domain, he says), husband Alan is a jovial, considerate host and works hard to ensure that guests feel comfortable and relaxed within his family home. He's also an excellent raconteur to boot – genuinely amusing – and enjoys sharing the kind of hidden-away detail about the surrounding area that you probably won't find in guide books or maps.

He's proud, too, of the folklore that is part of Dunvalanree. Built in 1938 the remote setting made it an attractive refuge for evacuees during the war. When Robert the Bruce landed at Port Righ in 1306, he stepped onto a stone that is now kept under the drawing room window of Carradale House (how do people *know* these things?) and whenever there was a north wind, the 40 or so boats that made up the Carradale fishing fleet used to shelter in Port Righ.

Most interesting, perhaps, in the context of the food that is served at Dunvalanree, is the intrinsically close relationship between the house and the local fishing industry. In the late 19th century, a certain Matthew McDougall moved from Torrisdale to Port Righ and built Lorne Cottage (ultimately to be demolished by his son to build Dunvalanree). From a large shed at the back of the cottage he started to build ring-net boats to catch herring. Whilst the shed is no more, the spout that supplied water to a boiler that was used to boil up bark for sealing the nets (a process called barking) is clearly visible at the bottom of the steep bank that leads down from Dunvalanree to the bay.

This is fabulous, tangible history that links Alan and Alyson with a heritage to which few others can lay claim. And whilst the herring boats are long gone, the sense of making good a living from the sea is still a strong one.

Salmon terrine with oak-smoked salmon and dill yoghurt dressing

An ideal starter or light lunch. This is an excellent summer dish. Use low fat crème fraîche instead of yoghurt if you prefer.

Serves 6

Ingredients

6 salmon fillets
1 pint/600ml of water and 1 glass (175ml) of dry white wine
Half a lemon
The juice and grated rind of 2 limes
Charred lime slices
4 tbs/60ml good quality mayonnaise
Whole peppercorns
Fresh dill
Tabasco sauce
Oak smoked salmon trimmings
Small carton of runny natural yoghurt into which a tablespoon of chopped dill is stirred

Method

Add the wine, whole half lemon, a tablespoon of peppercorns and a few sprigs of dill to the pint of water and pour this over the salmon fillets in an oven dish. Gently poach the salmon fillets for 8 minutes and remove from the liquor. (This can be reserved and used as fish stock or to make a roux to serve with pasta.)

Allow the fillets to cool and then flake up the flesh with a fork. Mix the fish with the mayonnaise, some chopped dill, the lime juice and rind and a dash of Tabasco.

To create the terrine, half fill a high-sided cookie cutter with the salmon mix, cover with some of the smoked salmon trimmings, then top with more of the salmon mix. Gently lift the cookie cutter from the terrine and chill the individual rounds in the fridge.

When ready to serve, place the terrines on plates, drizzle with the dill yoghurt and garnish with charred lime slices and some finely chopped dill.

Roast gigot of monkfish with garlic and rosemary

Like cod, monkfish is a hearty, flavoursome fish which responds well to robust pairings. Rosemary and garlic give this dish a distinctive edge, but sage would work well also.

Ingredients

4 monkfish tail fillets
4 cloves of garlic, thinly sliced
Olive oil
1 glass dry white wine
Maldon sea salt
Ground pepper

Method

Slash the flesh of the monkfish tails three or four times and fill each slash with garlic slices and fresh rosemary. Place the monkfish in a roasting tray and sprinkle with Maldon sea salt, pepper, olive oil and all of the white wine.

Cover and bake at 400°F/200°C for 10 minutes. Remove foil and check that fish is white and firm to the touch. Remove rosemary and replace with fresh sprigs. Put one fillet on each plate and pour over the remaining juices.

Garnish with a lemon wedge and some more fresh rosemary.

Fresh Haddock Rarebit

How easy is this! I like chunks of home-made bread to accompany this lunch/supper dish, but the slight sweetness of char-grilled brioche is also an excellent accompaniment. You can, of course, experiment with other cheeses, and swap the haddock for smoked haddock instead. In this instance, use a well-flavoured Mull cheddar to balance the smokiness of the fish.

Ingredients

4 large haddock fillets
Coarse grain Arran Mustard
7 oz/200g Campbeltown smoked cheddar, grated

Method

Place the haddock in a ceramic baking dish. Spread with Arran mustard and then cover with the grated cheese. Bake in a hot oven (400°F/200°C) until the cheese is melted and browned.

Serve with a green leaf salad and chunks of bread.

EE'USK

North Pier, Oban, Argyll PA34 5QD

T: +44 (0)1631 565666
E: eeusk.fishcafe@virgin.net
F: +44 (0)1631 570282
W: www.eeusk.com

'the minute you take your eye off the ball, or take anything for granted, the standards you've set start to slip'

In the far distance, across Oban Bay, the Isle of Kerrera lies in the mist, its single house silhouetted against the grey hills behind. Some hundred yachts tack and turn as they race downwind during West Highland Week – a spate of good weather has been replaced by a severe low pressure and the usually colourful sails look dulled and heavy with rain offshore.

Looming large, closer to shore, the Calmac's Lord of the Isles ferry berths against the quayside and the bustle of cars and passengers coming and going attracts the gaze of diners enjoying seafood within one of two contemporary glass tanks that houses ee'Usk. That's gaelic for fish. It's also smart, snazzy and sassy.

During the day attire is outdoor casual, as the weather dictates and despite the sense that you are, in fact, almost aboard a ship. A stainless-steel balcony adds another, casual, deck where diners can enjoy an aperitif, or read the dailies, or watch the ever-changing seascape. The higher vantage point lends to the sense of being afloat and after the odd glass or two of excellent, but moderately priced, wine you begin to believe that you are. Some tables are almost four-feet high and the more sprightly diners sit perched on bar-like stools, able to observe their fellow customers, the panoramic vista and the gleaming chrome and wood fittings in one eagle-eyed swoop.

It's not hard to imagine that it took Alan and Sheila McLeod five years to gain the planning permission required to turn two redundant and almost derelict harbour buildings into the stylish and predominantly transparent buildings that now take pride of place on Oban's North Pier. This is pure West End of Glasgow on the coast, and the traditionalists used to the 'tasteful' renovation of 19th-century seaside buildings must have initially struggled with the relatively industrial loft-style design that celebrates bringing the outside in and the inside out.

Oban's a funny place. If you've been in Scotland any length of time, you'll have been there at some point. Maybe you stayed in one of the willow-wallpapered guesthouses that served foil clad butter and jam portions with breakfast and tea with the fish supper at night. As a child, you might have strolled along the seafront and back again of an evening, treated to an ice cream before being packed off to bed by parents keen to have some time on their own. Oban is that kind of place. Very, very busy during the Easter and summer season, with a constant queue of traffic heading north or south through the town. Visitors are usually en route to the islands, or heading north to Fort William and Skye, or simply passing time when the rain falls. A large percentage of them are from overseas, and many have bypassed huge chunks of landscape simply to arrive at this gateway to the islands.

Oban's persona is, however, subtly shifting. The main street (can you have a main street when there's really only one?) now boasts an excellent delicatessen and wine shop. Ottakars provides a choice of books beyond mere local interest titles and while the woollen mills typically display exactly the same tartan kilts and travel rugs that you can buy in any tourist town from Inveraray to Pitlochry, it is now possible to buy slightly less outdated attire – if you know where to look.

But despite Oban's leap into the 21st century, the

Thai fishcakes with sweet chilli sauce

Sheila loves eastern spices and can happily get lost in some of Glasgow's Chinese groceries. Fresh coriander is critical, both for its flavour and wonderful colour.

Ingredients

1 lb/450g haddock or cod fillet (unboned)
2 lime leaves (dried) – available from Chinese grocers
1 tsp green Thai curry paste
1 red chilli, de-seeded and chopped
Groundnut oil
Fresh coriander
1 egg yolk, beaten, to bind

Method

Flake the haddock or cod by holding an upturned teaspoon in the palm of your hand with the thumb at the back of the spoon. Run the spoon down the middle of the fillet's length applying gentle pressure as you do so. This will separate the fish from the bone. Chop the lime leaves and add them with the rest of the ingredients, except the groundnut oil, to the fish and mix well until it all easily holds its shape.

Roll into balls and then flatten these slightly. Heat the groundnut oil in a wok and fry the fish balls a few at a time until they are cooked through (test with a skewer – if the skewer comes out clean, they're ready.)

Sweet chilli sauce

Sheila makes this in large quantities and then stores it in sterilised jam jars. A very versatile relish, this can make a great accompaniment to well-flavoured fish such as halibut, and as a dipping sauce for chilled langoustine.

Ingredients

12 large ripe tomatoes
3 green chilli peppers
2 large onions
2 tbs sugar
3 tsp apple cider vinegar
1 tbs cinnamon
1 tbs salt

Method

Peel the tomatoes by scoring the skins in four quarters with a sharp knife and steeping them in boiled water for two minutes. Remove them from the water with a draining spoon and allow them to cool. The skins can then be easily removed. Remove the seeds from the tomatoes and chop the remaining flesh. Chop the onions and chilli peppers and add these to the tomato. Mix well. Add the remainder of the ingredients and simmer gently for three to four hours, stirring frequently as it can stick to the bottom of the pan if not given due attention. When the relish is as thick as desired, pour it into clean jam jars sterilised with boiling water. Seal and use as required.

whole concept and design of ee'Usk remains a brave one. For a start, it's a large space to fill and whilst that's not too much of a concern during the honey-pot summer season, it's a reasonably realistic one during the winter. It's also, some would argue, a significant shift away from the rural restaurant with rooms that Alan, Sheila and son Callum previously took to a high standard over a 15-year period.

The McLeods moved from Glasgow to Port Appin in 1988 when they were successful in bidding 'way above the odds' for The Pier House – at that time a pub selling pub grub and not much else. They fell in love with the location and the style of the building – quaint, traditional and countrified. It took them five years to get into *The Good Food Guide*, and Sheila was, she admits, nervous at first to move beyond a menu that was traditional pub grub. Coming from Glasgow, she wasn't used to the abundance of fresh seafood and shellfish being delivered daily to her door. 'What on earth am I meant to do with these?' she remembers asking one fishermen who had kindly gifted her with a tray of writhing langoustines.

Sheila is undoubtedly the foodie of the family and has always cooked. She remembers making hundreds of cloutie dumplings as a youngster and selling them as part of a demonstration in John Lewis. Getting to grips with crustaceans, therefore, was simply another challenge to be overcome and she mastered the basics quickly and with flare. Her 15 years at the Pier House saw her build a business that pivoted around the reputation of the food, but getting to that standard was, it's clear, physically exhausting. She's keen to stress the long hours and 'graft' that is a prerequisite to gaining recognition with the food critics. 'The minute you take your eye off the ball, or take anything for granted, the standards you've set start to slip.' You sense a lady short on holidays.

When Alan and Sheila decided to sell up, Sheila assumed, hopefully, that quiet retirement was looming gently. Her husband and son Callum had other ideas and, after a year of what they now probably refer to as enforced retirement, began to develop plans on paper and in their heads for a restaurant that would build on the reputation they had amassed for themselves at the Pier House. Where she found the whole planning and funding process immensely stressful, Alan and Callum remained committed to their vision of being part of Oban's new, more contemporary, landscape. Ee'Usk was to be Oban's newest folly, and in many ways it now is.

Weary and in the middle of a very busy summer season, Sheila is now resigned to having less of a retirement than she might have wished for and travels from Port Appin every day to oversee the training of staff and the food service each evening. The menu is primarily hers – its simplicity lends itself to high-volume service and she takes great pride in being able to deliver this. Everything is locally sourced – oysters from Lismore; langoustines delivered daily to the kitchen door; and Robert (their invaluable jack of all trades) is tasked with daily visits to the fish pier to take their pick of the catch.

When the food arrives, it is a fabulous celebration of that rarely achieved combination of fish in optimum condition, cooked by people who have an intuitive feel for it. The lemon sole is magnificent grilled with lemon butter and peels easily from the bone yet holds its shape on the fork; a sure sign that it's been out of the water for less than a day. Roasted monkfish that has been seared first in a pan to achieve a bitter-sweet caramel crust, literally melts with flavour. You need to be hungry – really hungry – to do full justice to the Gruyère-rich lobster thermidor, but with a simple salad to go with it, this is soul food indeed.

The triumvirate of Sheila overseeing the kitchen, Alan dealing with the administration and son Callum out front, works well. And Callum is pure front-of-house; all easy charm and laid back affability – happy with the tortuous hours and driven by both passion and emotional sacrifice. You can tell that he was brought up in the trade, so to speak, not least because of the hours that he works, both in ee'Usk and in the Italian eatery that occupies the other glass cube next door. The clean, minimalist interior is also down to him and you sense a frustrated artist in his choice of oversized modernist canvasses placed carefully against otherwise bare walls.

There is very little wall space, in fact. Two thirds of the cube is glass and the back wall marginally screens the kitchen behind. Adornment comes mostly in the form of split levels with halogen chrome lighting crossing empty space to unite the whole. Cutlery and tableware is sleek, stylish, and Callum's service is a well-oiled machine, ultra-efficient and observant: human and personable.

Yachties in wellies. Londoners in linen. Ee'Usk has managed to pull off the relaxed ambience of a bistro with a feast of contemporary aesthetics that has wooed even the most die-hard traditionalists. And all with that constantly changing view that totally mesmerises you. And that's before you get to the menu.

Clam Chowder

If you're well organised you can poach salmon fillets for supper the night before. (One pint/600ml white wine to a cup of water is a good liquid balance.) The remaining liquor would work beautifully in this recipe.

Ingredients

2 oz/50g butter

1 oz/25g plain flour

12 shallots, finely chopped

12 whole scallops (roes included), quartered

1pt/600ml salmon stock (Sheila uses the poaching liquid from salmon cooked in the morning. Fish stock is OK, but dilute it slightly more than instructed.)

½ pt/300ml single cream

1 tbs/15ml brandy

1 spring onion – chopped finely

Method

Melt the butter in a wide, thick-based pan and sauté the shallots until soft. Remove the shallots and then add the scallops to the pan. Sear the scallops and the orange roes until browned on either side. (Do not overcook at this point as they will continue to cook when added to the warm stock.)

Remove the scallops and add the flour to the juices in the pan. Mix well until a soft roux is formed then slowly whisk in the brandy and then the salmon stock. Keep whisking all the time to avoid lumps forming.

Bring to the boil, turn down the heat, add the cream and simmer gently for 10 minutes. Keep warm until ready to serve.

When ready to serve add the scallops and shallots to the pan, reheat gently and serve garnished with some chopped spring onion and dill.

Lobster thermidor

Lobster thermidor is a rich dish that is said to have been named by Napoleon after the month in which he first tasted it. Thermidor was the 11th month of the Republican calendar which was used briefly after the French Revolution. The dish traditionally consists of lobster tail meat that has been cooked, removed from the shell, tossed with a bechamel sauce, topped with Parmesan cheese and then browned under a grill. Sheila's version is simpler and her adapted sauce goes beautifully with both crab and chicken.

Cooking lobster is incredibly easy and once you get the hang of removing the meat from their shell, putting it all back together again is straightforward. You could bypass this whole first stage by buying your lobster ready-cooked and chilled. Your fishmonger will be able to prepare it for you.

However, you do need a very large pan to cook live lobster and as they splash around a bit, you need to take care.

Ingredients
Two 1½-2 lb/675-900g live lobsters with claws firmly secured by elastic bands.
2 tbs/30ml white wine vinegar
Water to completely cover the lobsters

Method
Place the lobsters in a large stockpot or other similar container with a lid. Add the vinegar to the water in a pan that can be safely handled when full. Bring the water and vinegar to a rolling boil and then pour over the lobsters and cover.

Let the lobsters steep for two minutes for 1½ lb/675g lobsters and for three minutes for the 2 lb/900g lobsters. Remove the lobsters from the pot with tongs, twist off the claws with knuckles attached and return the claws to the pot for five minutes. During this time, plunge the lobsters into cold water. After five minutes remove the claws from the boiled, steeping water and add them to the lobsters in the pan of cold water.

Once the lobster and the claws are cold to the touch remove them from the water. Place each lobster on a large chopping board, shell side up. Take a large carving knife and plunge it into the centre of the head of the lobster and bring it down along the back of the shell. This effectively divides the body of the lobster in two, but you need to hold the head firmly with one hand, whilst you bring the knife down with the other.

Once each lobster is halved, remove the gut line and scrape out the dirty looking meat that is in the head piece; this can be saved and used for stock. Carefully, using a small sharp knife, remove the single piece of lobster flesh that fills each half of the body of the lobster. To remove the lobster meat from the claw, snip the elastic bands from each one and using a heavy wooden rolling-pin, hit the claw shell once, firmly. The shell should crack and you can then remove the shell fragments and extract the claw meat, again in one piece.

Sheila's thermidor sauce

Ingredients

4 tbs/60ml brandy
1pt/600ml double cream
2 oz/50g Gruyère cheese
2 oz/50g cheddar cheese
Dash of Worcestershire sauce
1 tsp English mustard
4 tbs grated parmesan
4 tbs breadcrumbs

Method

Bring the brandy to the boil and reduce by half. Be careful not to allow it to ignite over a gas hob. Add the double cream and bring to the boil again. Add both cheeses, stir well until the cheese has melted and then stir in the Worcestershire sauce and the mustard. Season lightly. Keep the sauce warm.

To assemble the finished dish, chop the lobster meat from the body into large chunks and add to the thermidor sauce. Spoon this mixture back into the four half-shells, saving just a little of the sauce to spoon over the claw meat, which should be placed, whole, in the head of the lobster.

Sprinkle over the parmesan and the breadcrumbs and fire under a hot grill until browned. Serve each half on a large plate with green salad and some chunky home-made fries.

Cairnbaan Hotel

By Lochgilphead, Argyll, PA31 8SJ

T: +44 (0)1546 603668
E: info@cairnbaan.com
F: +44 (0)1546 606045
W: www.cairnbaan.com

'some say that this is the most beautiful short-cut in Britain'

The Crinan Canal For Me by Alex MacKenzie

Oh! The Crinan Canal for me,
I don't like the wild raging sea,
It would be too terrific to cross the Pacific,
Or sail to Japan or Fiji.

A life on the Spanish Main,
I think it would drive me insane,
The big foaming breakers would give me the shakers,
It's the Crinan Canal for me.

Oh! The Crinan Canal for me,
I don't like the wild raging sea,
The big foaming breakers would give me the shakers,
It's the Crinan Canal for me.

It's the Crinan Canal for me,
From sea terrors there you are free,
There's no shark or whale that would make you feel pale,
Or shiver and shake at the knee.

I would nae like leavin' ma bones,
In a locker beside Davey Jones,
From Ardrishaig to Crinan's the best trip a'hve bin in,
The Crinan Canal for me.

CHORUS:

Aye the Crinan Canal for me,
It's neither too big nor too wee,
Oh it's lovely and calm when you're fryin' yer ham,
Or makin' a nice cup of tea.

You can go for a stroll on its banks,
To loosen your muscle bound shanks,
You can darn your socks while you're still in the locks,
The Crinan Canal for me.

OK, so it's yachts not steam boats and cars not carriages, but if you were to accompany Cairnbaan owner Darren Dobson on his daily dog-walking amble along the Crinan Canal, you might be forgiven for feeling that you have stepped back in time. Some say that this is the most beautiful shortcut in Britain. Nothing is rushed. Nothing much has changed. And the majority of people that you are likely to encounter simply while away the time. Meandering. Musing. Loosening their muscle-bound shanks.

Only a short nine miles (14.5km) long the Crinan Canal connects Ardrishaig on Loch Fyne with the Sound of Jura, and in so doing provides a navigable route between the Clyde and the Inner Hebrides. Without it craft would have to negotiate the 137-km journey north from the Clyde and through the potentially heavy seas off the Mull of Kintyre.

During the early 1800s it was primarily commercial vessels that made the slow journey through the 15 locks; it was actually quicker to walk! A healthy fishing fleet was able to easily traverse both sides of the peninsula to take advantage of plentiful fish stocks – some 500 boats alone were sporadically chasing the infamous Loch Fyne Herring. But in 1847, Queen Victoria and Prince Albert passed through on their way to a holiday in the Highlands, and this journey effectively kick-started a tourist revolution as thousands of people followed in their footsteps along what became known as 'The Royal Route.'

Well-documented photography of the time depicts the

canal in its early days: lock keepers would set up stall along the canal-side to sell an assortment of home-grown produce, and steamers dropped off and collected passengers at various points along the route. In the background of many of the photographs, standing proud in muted black and white, is the Cairnbaan Hotel, built in 1801 specifically to cater for the canal traveller.

According to Guthrie Hutton, author of *The Crinan Crinal*, the Cairnbaan Hotel was at one time ' … a temperance establishment, a situation today's drouthy boaters would regard as tantamount to cruelty.' Quite so.

And if it truly had been a 'Temperance establishment', it probably wasn't for very long. Today's avuncular owner Darren Dobson – a jolly, moustached, wine-loving gentleman whose bark is worse than his bite, prefers a somewhat more colourful history. It was once said that there was no crime or misdemeanour considered serious enough to have someone barred from the Cairnbaan Hotel, and goats and chickens often shared the bar. This tickles Darren's fancy and he chuckles in the telling. It's funnier still, given the lords and ladies, presidents and princesses who now frequent his hostelry.

Darren bought the Cairnbaan Hotel in 1999. Previously owner of the Montgreenan Mansion House Hotel in Irvine, his particular intention was to find a hotel that would provide his children with a safe rural upbringing. The Cairnbaan, in need of some gentle upgrading at the time of purchase, has proved an ideal choice, enabling him to build a business based on the excellence of the local produce.

Now, he couldn't imagine himself raising a family anywhere else – at seven and eight years old his son and daughter could cycle down the towpath to school and that is exactly how he hoped it would be.

Darren's wife, Christine, is the baker and starts work in the kitchen every morning at 4am, finishing five hours later, producing wonderful breads, puddings and pastries – her shortbread is renowned and morning coffee drinkers come a long way to enjoy it. Baking aside, Christine's early morning start enables her to spend the bulk of the day riding, either on her own or with her daughter who is doing exceptionally well in classical dressage en route to becoming an Olympian. Her

Lucitano breed, a Portuguese bull-fighting horse, can, according to Darren, stick its legs out a long way. You sense that Darren possibly writes the cheques more than he rides!

Darren's great passions are food, wine and travel and he is immensely proud of the fact that the Cairnbaan Hotel now boasts a solid single AA-rosette restaurant. Underpinning this accolade is a commitment to using only the best of local produce via suppliers who know him well. Like many other members of The Seafood Trail, he is frustrated that so much of the West coast's natural produce is exported to Spain and outraged at the price his Spanish counterparts charge for what they claim to be Spanish langoustines. 'I've sat in a Spanish restaurant and listened to the waiter extol the virtues of the local shellfish, knowing full well that his langoustines are delivered, live, from Scotland, every week. And I've ordered a portion of this supposedly Spanish delicacy only to find that two langoustines, cut into four tiny pieces, constitutes a main course. And the menu price? £18!'

His point, and it's a good one, is that somehow the Spanish market loves, and values, shellfish to a far great degree than its Scottish counterpart. And nobody seems to mind that shellfish exported from Scotland are branded as Spanish local produce. 'It's outrageous,' Darren argues. And you really have to agree.

So large blackboards displaying daily specials, both in the popular bar and in the conservatory, stress the freshness and the locality of the raw product – Loch Fyne lobster is from Loch Fyne. Langoustines are sometimes from the Sound of Jura, sometimes from Tarbert. Mussels are from Loch Etive. What you see is what you get.

The interior of the hotel is part-country house, part old-inn. The 11 bedrooms, a combination of twin and double, are luxurious. Squashy sofas downstairs are lethally comfortable and many a lunchtime diner has been gently lulled to sleep by the hypnotic passing of yacht masts only a few feet the other side of the road. Diners can settle in either the one-rosette restaurant, the busy bistro bar or the conservatory – the latter an excellent spot to enjoy a post-dinner liqueur or a coffee.

Guests staying at the hotel tend not to wander too far – the canal itself truly is a relic of another age, when travel was slower and the world a much bigger place. A gentle stroll along the canal bank takes you past the five Dunardy Locks, where the vista begins to open out onto Crinan Lock. Mid summer, with the mountainous island of Jura in the distance, a bright orange sun literally drops down onto the horizon and the colours of the sea and the sky are scorched and fiery.

The Cairnbaan's enviable position on the edge of the Crinan Canal is just part of its charm. The warm welcome, excellent local produce and genial owner Darren Dobson ever close to hand makes up the rest.

Goan Spiced Mussels

A change from moules marinières, this dish produces a wonderful aroma and can be served alongside a lightly seasoned basmati rice. Don't be put off by the relatively long list of ingredients. Once everything is prepared, the dish takes only ten minutes to cook. Try naan bread to dip into the juices, instead of crusty bread.

Ingredients

2 lb 4 oz/1kg cleaned and de-bearded mussels
3 tbs oil
5 cloves garlic, crushed
5-inch/125mm piece of fresh ginger, crushed
2 medium onions, finely chopped
3 red chillies, chopped (and de-seeded if you prefer mild to hot)
2 tsp ground cumin
2 tsp ground coriander
4 tomatoes, peeled, seeded and chopped
20 fl oz/500ml good fish stock
2 oz/50g fresh chopped coriander
2 tbs lemon juice

Method

Peel the tomatoes by scoring the skins in four quarters with a sharp knife and steeping them in boiled water for two minutes. Remove them from the water with a draining spoon and allow them to cool. The skins can then be easily removed. Remove the seeds from the tomatoes and chop the remaining flesh.

Heat the oil in a wok, add the garlic, ginger and onion and cook over a medium heat for 5 minutes. Add the chilli, cumin, ground coriander and tomatoes. Stir well and cook for 5 minutes

Add the mussels and the fish stock and bring to the boil. Reduce the heat, cover with the biggest lid you can find and simmer gently for another 5 minutes. Discard any unopened mussels.

Remove the wok from the heat and stir in the freshly chopped coriander and lemon juice.

Serve in deep bowls with added coriander for garnish.

Scallops with sauce vierge, creamed potatoes and crisp prosciutto

The crispy prosciutto adds both colour and texture to this simple dish. Use the best olive oil you can get for the sauce vierge and take the time to dice the tomatoes properly for a beautifully attractive dish. Sauce vierge also goes well with lobster and langoustines.

Serves Four

Ingredients
24 scallops, cleaned and trimmed
Plain flour for dusting
Olive oil
Prosciutto, frie or grilled until crisp

For the sauce vierge
3 tsp red wine vinegar
2 large shallots, peeled and finely chopped
4 cloves of garlic, peeled and finely chopped
10 fl oz/300ml good quality extra virgin olive oil
8 medium tomatoes: skinned, cored, seeded and diced
A handful of fresh basil leaves, roughly torn

Method
To make the sauce vierge
Peel the tomatoes by scoring the skins in four quarters with a sharp knife and steeping them in boiled water for two minutes. Remove them from the water with a draining spoon and allow them to cool. The skins can then be easily removed. Remove the seeds from the tomatoes and dice the remaining flesh. Reserve.

Pour the vinegar into a bowl, stir in the garlic and chopped shallots. Leave this mixture to infuse for a minimum of two hours. Just before serving, whisk in the olive oil, stir in the diced tomatoes and the torn basil. Season with salt and pepper.

To cook the scallops
Place a heavy-bottomed pan over a very high heat. Season the scallops, then dust them lightly with flour. Smear both sides of the scallops with olive oil and sear them in the pan for 1 minute on each side.

To serve
Arrange the scallops around a pile of creamy mash (made with good floury potatoes) and drizzle with the sauce vierge.

Place the crisp prosciutto on top of the mash and enjoy.

Salmon and smoked haddock fishcakes with saffron and smoked mussel cream

Fishcakes are a wonderfully warming, familiar dish, but don't skimp on the ingredients here. The chef gets his haddock locally – it's lightly smoked and has no artificial colouring and this ensures that the more delicate salmon isn't overpowered.

Be careful not to 'cook' the smoked mussels. They're already cooked (you can buy them in tins or small jars from most good supermarkets and delicatessens (remember to drain them well) and to ensure a texture that isn't rubbery, you need only warm them through in the cream.

Ingredients

8 oz/240g salmon fillet
8 oz/240g pale-smoked haddock
12 peppercorns
2 bay leaves
Milk to cover
7 oz/200g Maris Piper potatoes – cooked and mashed with butter
Chopped chives and flat parsley
Juice of half a lemon
Salt and pepper
Flour to coat fishcakes
2 eggs beaten
4 oz/100g breadcrumbs (made from day-old bread)
Flat leaf parsley

For the fishcakes

Poach the salmon and smoked haddock in the milk along with the bay leaves and peppercorns. Remove the fish, flake into bite-sized pieces and mix with all the other ingredients.

Shape the mixture into rounds, dip in the flour, the beaten egg and finally the breadcrumbs.

Shallow fry the fishcakes until golden-brown in a mixture of oil and butter, turning once.

For the saffron and smoked mussel sauce

7 fl oz/200ml good quality fish stock
15 fl oz/425ml double cream
A good pinch of saffron threads
A handful of smoked mussels
Lemon juice to taste

Dissolve the saffron in a little hot stock and leave for at least ten minutes to infuse. Add the rest of the stock to a saucepan, bring to the boil and reduce. Add the cream and saffron and reduce again. Finally, throw in the smoked mussels and gently warm them through, adding lemon juice to taste.

Serve the fishcakes in a pool of the saffron sauce, garnished with flat-leafed parsley.

Laroch Foods

Clachan, Tarbert, Argyll PA29 6XN

T: +44 (0)1546 600391
E: sales@larochfoods.co.uk
F: +44 (0)1546 600391
W: www.larochfoods.co.uk

'Tove's existence blends old with new'

Dressed casually in sweatshirt, jeans and a large colourful sailing jacket, Tove Knight appears somewhat distracted as we discuss how she came to live in Kintyre. England have just won the Ashes and she is keen to be home by lunchtime in order to catch the cricket highlights on TV; she'll watch them again in the evening. And possibly catch the late-night round-up on the radio before going to bed. Married to a cricket-loving Scotsman who played rugby for Norway in its first ever international, Tove leads an absolutely contented life, and one which is as far removed from her career in the oil industry as you might ever imagine. Yet her journey to Kintyre has its beginnings in a life closely associated with the oceans and her purchase of a small online food delivery business isn't the anomaly that at first it might seem.

Born right above the Arctic Circle in Norway, she was raised by parents who owned and ran a small shipyard. Growing up, Tove sensed that she would enter a similar field and moved to Newcastle after her A levels to study naval architecture. Whilst there she met her husband Ron, and they returned to Norway to find jobs in the oil industry.

Both missed the UK, however – particularly the cricket – and loathed the harsh, dark sunless days that started on the 21st November and ended on the 20th January, precisely (or thereabouts!), according to Tove. It was also difficult for Ron to progress when he was not 'of that nation', and a move to London in 1981 was followed by another location shift, this time to Aberdeen and to a key job for her as operations manager for a new gas pipeline going into Shetland. Much of Tove's time was, consequently, spent offshore on rigs and production vessels and on-the-job time was intensive.

Sanctuary was a yacht in Ardfern, at the head of Loch Craignish and one of Scotland's most beautiful and sheltered sea lochs. While exploring some of the small islands dotted nearby, conversation would often turn to where might become their permanent base and Tove's preference, always, was for somewhere between Lochgilphead and Oban.

In the end, their move brought them further south, to Clachan – a tiny hamlet some third of the way down the west Kintyre peninsula, south of Tarbert. Finding a plot of land with views south across a forested landscape was the perfect opportunity to build the house they had always dreamt of and Tove's design drew much from the timber-framed, energy-efficient houses prevalent in Norway.

It took five years to build the house, during which time Tove took redundancy from BP and worked for a short time in local enterprise. But with a fabulous house located in a captivating spot, her preference was to work from home. Opportunity presented itself when a friend suggested she buy Laroch Foods – suppliers of premier quality, traditionally smoked salmon, fish, cheese and meats from Scotland.

With Norwegian roots, Tove is a great lover of smoked products, and at game fairs and food festivals speaks knowledgeably with prospective customers, not just about the fish, but about the traditional processes that bring about such diverse flavours. Smoked trout is her personal favourite – it's dryer than salmon, she says, but more delicate in flavour; less strongly smoked than its cousin salmon tends to be. Smoked eel is becoming more popular: the initial reaction is slightly off-putting, but Tove finds that everyone who tries it loves the robust meatiness of it. At home, she serves a small amount as a starter, perhaps with a fruity mango and avocado salsa. It is also good as a cold main course with hollandaise sauce and warm new potatoes.

Another favourite is smoked swordfish – again delicate in flavour – but a product that benefits from being offered as a taster first. According to Tove, we have very particular tastes when it comes to smoked products; interesting given that in the days preceding refrigeration and canning smoking fish and meat was much more about preserving the product than it was about delicate flavours on the palate. In Europe and Britain during the Middle Ages, various heavily smoked and salted foods were relied upon to carry people over the lean times of late winter and into spring. Fresh fish could not be transported any distance from the port of landing unless preserved, and in the 1800s, along the length of the Kintyre coast and in Loch Fyne, herring and cod were trawled, netted and smoked in abundance – the Loch Fyne kipper (smoked herring) is still universally popular as a breakfast delicacy.

With the advent of the railways it became possible to move perishables more quickly from the quayside to the city markets. This effectively marked the beginning of the industrialisation of sea fishing. As a result of the widespread availability of fresh fish, the popularity of heavily salted, heavily smoked products – a mainstay for hundreds of years – began to decline. During the same period (mid-1800's), the smoked fish products we now regard as traditional came into being as the main reason for smoking fish was now mainly to impart a pleasant, mild, smoky flavour.

Traditional smoking, sometimes referred to as cold-smoking, is part of a painstaking process that relies heavily on the quality of the raw produce. Fish is filleted first, then steeped in a mixture of salt and sugar along with whatever spices are favoured by particular smokers. The brining process itself can take between 12 and 24 hours: the salt and sugar solution must completely saturate the fish in order to extract the moisture retained naturally in the flesh, thereby minimising potential bacterial activity and spoilage. The solution is then rinsed off and the fish refrigerated for up to 12 hours – the final stage in the curing process and one which ensures that the salt that is left is distributed evenly throughout the flesh of the fish.

It is only at this stage that the actual smoking begins. The basics of cold smoking are that the smoker should never be hotter than 80°C and that the smoker is used to colour and flavour the item being smoked but never to thermally cook it. Cold-smoked products are still raw when we eat them – unlike hot-smoked products which are cooked thermally whilst at the same time gaining flavour and colour from the smoke – in hot-smoking the temperature is usually above 170°C.

Whichever kind of smoking – hot or cold – you need a source of heat and smoke, a chamber in which the food is smoked and a source of air. The air enters at the bottom of the device, mingles with the fuel source creating smoke that is vented through to the smoking chamber imparting a smoky flavour to the food. Here it draws off some of the moisture and exits through a vent. At the

end of the process, the food has picked up the smoky flavour and been dried somewhat.

Not surprisingly, the choice of fuel for smoking varies a great deal with geography. Some smokehouses use peat; some use whisky barrel shavings; others advocate the use of more resinous woods with oilier fish like mackerel to counter the strong taste. Most reputable smokers spurn the use of softwoods in favour of hardwoods: wood smoke is composed of millions of microscopic particles which rise like a fog that is mostly water, carbon and trace solids. The vapour contains what smokers are after, namely volatile oils which are released from the wood and furnish the characteristic flavours and preservative qualities.

So smoking is an art, Tove contends, steeped in tradition and folklore and well guarded secret recipes. You can buy the greasy, rubbery, brightly coloured mass produced stuff in most large supermarkets but her customers, at least, are happy to pay a premium for superlatively differ-ent produce. In fashion terms, delicately smoked seafood is the aficionado's equivalent of haute couture.

And what does Tove do when she's not running her mail order business? Does she miss her previous corporate life, offshore and overseas? Apparently not; she's moved around so much, she says, that she rarely looks back and doesn't artificially try to keep in touch with her old life. There seems little point when she loves her life here – sailing, taking the dogs for a walk and meeting nothing but deer, watching cricket, socialising with good friends – in short, becoming, at last, part of a community. Even enjoying the visits by the local doctor to his makeshift surgery in the local church. 'You take a pew and wait to be called,' she chuckles, enjoying the uniqueness of it all.

Tove's existence blends old with new. Traditionally prepared produce dispatched by mail from a home office in the middle of nowhere – linked to the rest of the world by technology ... and a passion for food.

Salad of smoked halibut & smoked eel

An imaginative but unusual combination. The halibut is very delicate and the eel quite meaty, so you need less of the latter and more of the former! Both blend very well with the crispy fried bacon. This can be used as a starter or, by adding some bread and butter or warm potato salad, it can be turned into a delightful lunch or supper. Serves six as a starter, or four for lunch or supper.

Ingredients

7 oz/200g smoked halibut fillet
4 oz/100g smoked eel fillets
5 oz/150g smoked bacon
5 fl oz/150ml double cream (or half cream/half yoghurt or crème fraîche)
2 tbs of horseradish sauce (or dill mustard sauce if you prefer)
Juice from 1 lemon
Approx 5 oz/150g of mixed crispy salad leaves
Salt and pepper to taste

3 chopped sundried tomatoes
3 tbs of chopped chives

Method

Remove the rind and grill the bacon rashers until very crisp. Drain and cool. Break into bite-sized pieces.

Warm the cream slowly (do not boil) and mix in the horseradish or dill mustard sauce. Add lemon juice and season.

Cut the fish into bite-sized bits. Arrange the salad leaves on individual serving plates, add the fish with the bacon on top. Spoon over some dressing.

Sprinkle the chives and sundried tomatoes over the top. Serve with warm potato salad or brown bread and butter to make this in to a supper or lunch dish.

Smoked cod roe on toast

The beauty of using smoked products is that they can involve next to no preparation time whatsoever and are a great way of ensuring that you always have something to hand for guests who simply drop by. This recipe, using smoked cod roe is a deliciously light example of precisely that and works well as a quick snack or unusual starter.

Serves two as a main or four as a starter.

Ingredients

3 tbs of cream or crème fraîche
1 oz/30g butter
1 tsp lemon juice
1 tsp English mustard
1 shallot or half a small onion
1 small bunch parsley, chopped
1 smoked cod roe approx 7 oz/200g
4 slices good white bread
1 pinch paprika
Rocket salad leaves (optional)

Method

Put the double cream, butter, lemon juice, mustard, shallot and parsley into a saucepan and heat together. Bring to the boil and remove from heat.

Add the cod roe and mix thoroughly.

Toast the bread.

Spread a generous portion of the cod roe mixture over the toast and sprinkle with paprika.

Serve with a dressed rocket salad (optional).

Smoked salmon and dill soup

The flavours in this soup alter according to how the salmon has been smoked – you can experiment with oaked or peat-smoked, for instance, and instantly sense a difference. Malt whisky is used here to add depth, and it would seem obvious to go for one of the more smoky Islays, such as Ardbeg, Lagavulin or Laphroaig, but a good splash of dry white wine would work also. This is a luxurious soup with a lovely colour. Serves four. Enjoy.

Ingredients

1 fl oz/25ml olive oil
2 shallots, finely chopped
1 large potato, cubed
25 fl oz/750ml chicken stock
Generous handful of chopped fresh dill
10 oz/300g of smoked salmon, flaked
2 fl oz/50ml double cream
2 fl oz/50ml malt whisky
salt
Freshly ground black pepper
Chopped flat leaf parsley
1 tbs single cream (optional)

Method

Gently cook the shallots in the olive oil for a few minutes until translucent. Add the cubed potato, 4 oz/100g of the smoked salmon and the stock and bring to the boil. Reduce the heat and simmer for about 20 minutes.

Add the dill, stir well and allow the soup to cool. Blend in a food processor until smooth, then add the remaining smoked salmon, the cream, the malt whisky and the seasoning.

Reheat the soup slowly before serving and serve garnished with the chopped parsley and a swirl of cream if preferred.

The Royal at Tighnabruaich

Kyles of Bute, Argyll, PA21 2BE

T: +44 (0)1700 811239
E: info@royalhotel.org.uk
F: +44 (0)1700 811300
W: www.royalhotel.org.uk

'For sheer, unadulterated full-on cosseting, look no further'

Two short letters of formally headed correspondence are displayed to the side of the mosaic-floored entrance to The Royal, Tighnabruaich. The first begins: 'My attention has been drawn to the fact that in the 29th October issue of the Sunday Herald Travel Magazine you advertised your hotel as serving venison caught by Winston Churchill. If indeed this be so it must, by now, be very high indeed!'

Roger Mckie's written reply asserts: ' ... our venison is not at all high, but absolutely delicious. All our fish and game is sourced locally. Venison is stalked and butchered by Winston Churchill. Winston operates from a purpose-built site on the edge of Dunoon. I have asked him to send you some venison with our compliments.'

And here's the point. Owners Roger and Bea Mckie, and their young talented chef – daughter Louise – have shifted away from the traditional West-coast tendency towards fuss and frippery to focus purely on the provenance of the very best local produce. They not only know where their fresh produce comes from geographically, they also know who caught it, how they caught it, and when they are likely to get more. Scallops are hand-dived by Mary; Arthur plucks the langoustines from The Kyles of Bute (first names only, apparently); wild salmon is smoked in Tighnabruaich by a local Swiss resident; and venison is indeed stalked by a Mr Winston Churchill. When you are as proud of, and familiar with, your suppliers as the McKie's clearly are, it's likely that the food is going to be exceptional, not for what you have to do to it, but for what you don't.

So, if you're a visitor to The Royal you arrive with high expectations thanks to a growing reputation amongst food critics, a chef who knows how to make the basics taste exactly as they should and owners, Roger and Bea and their other two daughters, Claire and Katie, who, collectively, have immersed themselves in the creation of what must now surely be one of Scotland's most enviously stylish, comfortable and discreet, water's edge hotels.

The location helps, of course. Overlooking the Kyles of Bute towards the unpopulated coast of Bute itself, The Royal sits to the outer edge of Tighnabruaich – a sleepy village that hugs the gentle coast and boasts its own art gallery, coffee shop and sailing school. The long promenade that starts at the Royal and ends a short walk away at the boat yard is lined on one side by mostly traditional stone built villas and on the other by a narrow stretch of water that is a popular channel for sailors heading for the Western Isles. Yet even the tide is respectful of the peaceful ambience here, tiptoeing up the beach to rest before backtracking out to sea, leaving behind just enough shingle sand to enjoy a picnic on the shore or a game of skimming stones.

The Royal looks royal – clearly visible from both the water and the shore, its whitewashed walls are punctuated by well dressed windows; an understated conservatory built recently to take advantage of the views beyond looks comfortably aged. Inside, however, the interior is bold. Traditionally earthy Scottish colours feature throughout. Strong reds and muddy greens – inspired by the Scottish landscape no doubt – are favourites and create the ambience of a relaxed country house. More contemporary cream furnishings however, nice touches like the driftwood mirror that dou-

bles the length and impact of the short hallway to the cloakrooms, and the rich, heavily painted canvasses that embellish every wall, testify to a traditional feel with a decidedly modern twist. Roger and Bea Mckie have a strong sense of style.

On a summer's day it is impossible not to be drawn to the front of the hotel, where the romantic dining room (The Crustacean), and the lively brasserie (The Deck), afford outstanding views across the water. Yachtsmen hooking one of the Royal's private moorings row ashore to enjoy breakfast, lunch or dinner and guests enjoy watching this burst of activity on an otherwise tranquil landscape. The relaxed bar area, with its huge fireplace to the side, is dangerously comfortable – books of local interest are within easy reach; good food guides; walks and wildlife references. Paintings by renowned local artists tempt you to sit and rest your eyes and the abundantly simple menu encourages those with the luxury of time on their hands to sample Arthur's langoustines, perhaps, or Mary's scallops or a carpaccio of Winston Churchill's venison.

Backstage the kitchen is gleaming stainless steel and white tiles – a purpose built professional work space to replace the mishmash of equipment that the Mckies inherited when they purchased the run-down building some eight years previously. A kitchen designed to be taken seriously, and one in which 22-year-old Louise McKie spent almost a year and a half persuading her father that she wanted to work. Roger spent equally as long encouraging her to focus front of house. But a passion for cooking that had developed as a youngster, juxtaposed with foodie parents and a sister, Claire, who had already won the Royal its first AA Rosette were credentials that Roger could not easily ignore.

Working closely with sister Claire and father Roger – both passionate and self-taught chefs – Louise quickly amassed the Royal way: keep things simple, don't overcomplicate with too many flavours and let the quality of the local produce shine through. A keen understanding of basic techniques followed and her first-rate mayonnaise, well balanced stocks and delicately flavoured vinaigrettes now coax the best from raw ingredients. Louise also makes her own pasta – her seafood tagli-

atelle won two rosettes – finding the whole process, like bread-making, hugely therapeutic.

Nominated already for a number of awards, including Scottish Chef's 'Best Rural Chef of 2005' award, and keenly sought after by programme makers and journalists recognising a rising chef, Louise remains steadfastly committed to cooking. She is modest about her own skills, but speaks confidently and comfortably about what works in her kitchen and what doesn't. Here is a chef who is self-taught, obsessive, enthralled by taste. When photographers drop by, she is reluctant to leave the kitchen for long: there are no shortcuts and taking the time to get the preparation right early in the day is critical to the dishes that are ultimately delivered front of house.

Royal menus read prosaically: Tighnabruaich smoked salmon, red onion caper cream, mock caviar. Trio of shellfish: squat lobsters, mussels, grilled oysters. For meat lovers: game terrine, truffle oil, olive toasts; venison stalked by Winston Churchill of Dunoon: venison fillet, pearl barley & venison sausage risotto, kurly kale. There are no convoluted descriptions, or even much detail about cooking methods, so the impact – when the food arrives – is all the greater. Beautifully fresh food, prepared with a precise attention to the basics.

This family-run business is unique, not least because its individual members remain so collectively committed to the highest of standards. Bea's skill as an interior designer is exemplified by the way the Royal works as a whole, but she also leads a front-of-house team who value the care of the guest above all else. Roger, sometimes chef, sometimes businessman, is guided and always has been, by a very clear vision of how he wants the Royal to be, and is hugely proud that all three of his daughters now play important roles in the overall running of the hotel.

Eldest daughter Claire, now a partner in the business, takes charge of the recently opened Café Royal in Glasgow's West End (Broomhill) and has already won an AA rosette for a menu which benefits from access to some of the best Scottish produce available, all served with the same attention to detail, albeit via a smaller menu, as its parent, The Royal. ('An outpost of the west coast in the heart of the city', according to Sunday Times food writer, Allan Brown.) Middle daughter, Louise – also now a partner in the business, enjoys Tighnabruaich's more rural landscape and looks forward to the onset of winter – a time to experiment with flavours and ideas in advance of the next busy summer season. Youngest daughter, Katy has also joined the family firm – liasing between both establishments and organising front of house in Glasgow.

Everything about The Royal is wonderful: the food, the setting, the ambience and the people who work there. For sheer, unadulterated full-on cosseting, look no further.

Scallops, monkfish, tagliatelle, pea and parsley velouté

This might appear somewhat fiddly, but the end result is a wonderful combination of flavour and texture. Of course, you don't have to make your own tagliatelle – but if you are buying ready made, use the fresh tagliatelle that you can find in the chilled section of most supermarkets.

Ingredients
1 lb/450g monkfish tail, cut into 2.5cm/1-in pieces
12 large scallops
Butter

For the pasta
1lb/450g '00' brand flour, 5 eggs, seasoning, 1 tbs olive oil

Method
Whizz the ingredients in a food processor. Knead the resultant dough well and allow it to rest for 1 hour in the fridge. Roll it out using a pasta machine and then feed the dough in and cut it with the tagliatelle attachment. Hang the tagliatelle to dry for 20 minutes.

For the velouté
Ingredients
1pt/600ml fish stock and white wine, comprising 50/50 of each
1pt/600ml double cream

Method
Reduce the wine/stock mix in a thick-based pan over a fierce heat to 50% of its original volume and then add the double cream, stirring until the sauce is velvety.

Add a knob of butter to a hot frying pan. Pan fry the monkfish until just cooked. Remove from the pan, add another knob of butter and caramelise the scallops once the butter is sizzling. Cook the fresh pasta in boiling salted water for five minutes.

Add some chopped parsley and petit pois to the velouté and a pinch of saffron to soften the colour if you like. Whisk this to create a frothy sauce.

Drain the pasta and mix with the monkfish in a deep bowl. Add the velouté, peas and parsley and arrange the scallops. Serve steaming hot in wide generous bowls for maximum effect.

Seasonal fruit tatin

These little fruit tatins are incredibly easy to make. If using nectarines or plums or peaches, make sure the fruit is not too ripe otherwise the high heat will reduce them to mush. The puff pastry should be draped over the fruit and roughly cut to size. The alcohol added to the caramel mixture should suit the fruits – cider with apple; a nice muscat with peaches.

Ingredients
Seasonal fruit: pears, apples, nectarines, plums etc

Method
Cut the chosen fruit in half. Coat the uncut side with egg wash and cover with puff pastry. Set aside and chill for 30 minutes.

For the caramel mixture
5 oz/150g caster sugar
4 oz/125g butter
Seeds from 1 vanilla pod
1 fl oz/25ml alcohol

Method
Saturate the sugar in a little water for 10 minutes. Place the sugared water in a thick-bottomed pan over a low heat, moving the pan occasionally until dissolved.

Increase the heat and cook to a medium-brown caramel. (Do not leave the pan unattended at this point as the mixture can easily burn and stick to the inside of the pan.)

Remove from heat, stand the pan to one side and after one minute add the butter, vanilla seeds and alcohol. Pour the caramel into individual oven-proof dishes (crème brulée dishes for instance) and place the fruit on top, pastry-side-up.

Put in a 210°C/400°F oven for 15 minutes until the pastry is brown.

Remove and serve.

West coast langoustines with home-made garlic mayonnaise*

Once you realise how easy it is to make your own mayonnaise, you'll wonder why you never did it before. The trick is to add the oil very, very, slowly while still whisking the egg mixture. A food processor is ideal for this. The mayonnaise can then be flavoured with freshly-chopped herbs to instantly change the nature of a dish.

Ingredients
6 langoustines per person
A large pot of boiling salted water (or seawater!)

Method
Immerse the langoustines in the water. The water will cease boiling, but as soon as it returns to the boil remove the langoustines and place them in cold water to stop the cooking process.

Arrange the langoustines on the serving plates with lemon wedges, parsley and a generous dollop of the mayonnaise.

For the mayonnaise
2 egg Yolks
2 cloves of crushed garlic
1 tsp Dijon mustard
Pinch of caster sugar
1 tsp hot water
2 fl oz/50ml olive oil mixed with 2 fl oz/50ml sunflower oil in a measuring jug
Lemon juice to taste

Method
Whizz the egg yolks in a food processor. Slowly trickle in the mixture of oils until the mayonnaise starts to thicken. Add the lemon juice, sugar and mustard together. Add the rest of the oil slowly.

When all the oil is added, add the hot water and crushed garlic. Allow to cool and it is ready to serve.

*Mayonnaise was first created on the island of Menorca in the Balearics 250 years ago. The island was fiercely contested by the French and British due to Mahon's huge natural harbour. After Admiral Byng failed to relieve the garrison in May 1756, the Duc de Richelieu claimed the island for France once more. His chef created a victory feast that was to include a sauce made of cream and eggs. As there was no cream available, the Duc's chef substituted olive oil. He named the new sauce 'Mahonnaise' in honour of the Duc's victory. Curiously, the British eventually re-captured Menorca and imported dairy cattle so a lack of cream became unlikely in the future! Admiral Byng returned to England, was court-martialled and shot.

The Loch Fyne Oyster Bar

Cairndow, Argyll PA21 2BE

T: +44 (0)1499 600236
E: oysterb@lochfyne.com
F: +44 (0)1499 600234
W: www.lochfyne.com

'Nach Urramach An Cuan – *how worthy of honour is the sea'*

It's not surprising that by the time you've arrived at The Loch Fyne Oyster Bar you're craving the mollusc that gave it its name. Deceptively close to Glasgow as the crow flies, the journey edges much of the length of Loch Lomond, skirts the top end of Loch Long and then tortuously climbs the winding pass of Rest and Be Thankful through the Arrochar Alps and up Glen Croe.

At the top of the pass, look back down the valley as the view empties; on a clear day, sharp peaks serrate the skyline and disgorging waterfalls plummet through the dramatic backdrop. When clouds veil the rugged landscape, they dim what the eye can see yet they help to turn up the sound control so that teeming rainfall sounds like a deluge.

Coming down the other side of the pass is easier. The road still twists and winds; snow poles either side betray the fierceness of winter on this shadowed landscape and the scarred hillsides bear testament to the law of nature that states that water will always find the quickest route down. But this is a gentler descent towards Loch Fyne and the eponymous eaterie that sits on its far shore. As one tabloid commentator observed: 'Not quite in the middle of nowhere, but still a long walk from somewhere.'

Of course, you don't have to be an oyster fan to enjoy The Loch Fyne Oyster Bar, although its something of a shame if you're not. Giant oyster beds, seeded back in 1978, sit a couple of miles away at Ardkinglas Bay, feeding lazily on plankton brought in by the sea loch's tidal streams. The clean waters also provide an ideal breeding ground for mussels, and Loch Fyne now has some 18 miles of mussel ropes.

Greta Cameron is the company's longest standing employee. Now the Oyster Bar Director, she remembers humbler beginnings: 'Andy Lane, our surviving founder, sold oysters and fresh fish from a small table set up by the side of the loch. He moved his operation to where we are now in order to establish a smokehouse and a shop and I was put in charge of what we described, then, as the picnic area. We sold oysters and smoked salmon sandwiches and somewhat grandly called ourselves The Oyster Bar. A lot of people laughed at that.'

Laugh they might, but within half an hour of opening, The Oyster Bar was packed. 'On the back of our success, we decided to expand our repertoire somewhat,' Greta explains. 'We served boiled potatoes, and cooked langoustines in a shed at the back. At the end of every season, we had to buy more equipment, employ more people and add more space.'

And more space ... and more space. Now the sprawling, low slung building houses a shop and a restaurant that juts off at a right angle into the barns behind. Yet the philosophy remains intact: to serve top quality seafood and shellfish, produced from sustainable sources, in relaxed and friendly surroundings.

The issue of sustainability is a critical one, not least because being so close to natural produce is a privilege that should be neither over-exploited nor overlooked, according to Virginia Sumsion, PR Manager and niece of the late Johnny Noble. 'Given the urgent issues facing seafood resources, our over-riding principle is to leave the environment undamaged and to work towards improving the overall marine landscape,' she says.

If you think that this is a somewhat grandiose ethos, judge the actions, not the words. The restaurant's

salmon comes from The Sustainable Salmon Company at Loch Duart. This particular fishery is based on the far north-west of Scotland, where the cold, clear Atlantic waters offer a self-generating, pollution-free environment providing the perfect conditions for rearing salmon of exceptional quality. The salmon is then smoked at the Loch Fyne Smoke House using traditional methods.

Clearly, Virginia is not a subscriber to what she describes as fish snobbery, and would not dream, for instance, of eating wild salmon. 'It's an endangered species. Why would I?' she challenges.

It actually doesn't matter whether you subscribe to this line of thinking or not; the crowded lunchtime restaurant attracts visitors from around the globe, regardless. The Loch Fyne Oyster Bar is now something of an institution; visitors from the nearby Glasgow suburbs mingle with Japanese and Scandinavian holiday-makers, browsing the eclectic collection of arts and sea-related artefacts that adorn the whitewashed walls before coming to rest on benches and seats that are a tad more practical than comfortable.

Once seated, the menu promises simple pleasures – Bradan Rost salmon paté; Loch Fyne kippers; queenies served raw with lime. This is cooking stripped bare, the true test being the quality of the raw ingredients. Oysters are mechanically opened by a one-armed gadget that in one downward pull separates the shells to reveal the meaty fish within. The house-smoked salmon has a faint aroma of whisky, thanks to the whisky barrel shavings used to fire the kilns housed in the barn at the back of the restaurant. If sometimes you have to wait a while, it's probably because the lobster claw is proving difficult to crack, or because the cullen skink hasn't yet reached its characteristically rich and creamy flavour.

Waiting, here, is simply an interlude. An opportunity to watch your fellow diners – a young Japanese family intent on extracting every last morsel from their three-tiered shellfish platter; an elderly tweed-clad couple debating the choice of wine.

Nach Urramach An Cuan – how worthy of honour is the sea. It's not a mantra you're likely to forget as you wind your way back home.

Oysters Rockefeller

Oysters Rockefeller are said to have originated in Antoine's Restaurant in New Orleans. Their recipe is a closely guarded secret, but here is an approximation of their most famous dish.

Serves six.

Ingredients
6 tbs butter
3 tbs parsley (minced)
Tabasco sauce (dash)
½ tsp salt
36 fresh oysters (on the half shell)
6 tbs raw spinach (finely minced)
5 tbs fresh breadcrumbs
½ tsp Herbsaint (or Pernod)

Method
Melt the butter in a saucepan, adding all the ingredients except the oysters. Cook constantly for 15 minutes.

Cool the mixture enough to handle it then pass it through a food mill or mince finely by hand. Fill a shallow baking tray with rock salt and set the open oysters in the salt. Divide the topping between all the oysters and grill on high until the topping is brown.

Loch Fyne Bradan Rost
with whisky sauce

Bradan Rost (roasted salmon in Gaelic) is smoked at ambient temperatures for 12 hours before extra fire boxes are lit and the fillets cooked through. It is this unique double process that gives the fish such a succulent, moist, flaky texture and a mild smoky flavour. Thickly sliced, Bradan Rost is ideal as a starter, or as a main meal, served with a creamed horseradish sauce. It also makes an impressive hot dish, warmed through gently in the oven and served with this delicious whisky sauce.

For the whisky sauce
250ml crème fraîche
1 tbs creamed horseradish sauce
1 tbs whisky*
Lemon juice
Black pepper

Method
Mix the crème fraîche, horseradish and whisky in a small thick-bottomed pan and heat through very gently. Add the lemon juice and black pepper to taste. Pour the sauce over the salmon and serve with new potatoes or crusty bread and a crisp green salad.

*A straight blend is fine. For a more pungent sauce use an Islay malt such as Lagavulin or Laphroaig.

Pan-fried fillet of sea bass with artichokes and rosemary

This is summer personified and the rosemary perfectly compliments the earthiness of the potatoes and olives in this rustic dish.

Ingredients

2 tsp/10ml olive oil
4 oz/100g shallots, finely chopped
1 clove of garlic, finely chopped
3 fl oz/100ml white wine
8 oz/250g new potatoes
3 oz/80g Kalamata olives
1 tin of artichokes, drained
1 sprig of rosemary
12 cherry tomatoes
1 whole seabass, filleted

Method

Boil the new potatoes until tender. Drain, cool and halve. Heat the olive oil in a sauté pan and add the shallots and garlic. Cook gently until the shallots begin to soften, then add the white wine and reduce the heat. Drain the artichokes, squeezing out any excess liquid, and cut them into quarters. Add these to the shallots and garlic along with the olives and potatoes. Strip the rosemary leaves from the stalk and chop very finely. Add this to the sauce with the halved cherry tomatoes.

Meanwhile, divide each seabass fillet, creating two diamond shapes. Heat a griddle until very hot. Brush each fillet with olive oil and char-grill, skin side down, until cooked with a crispy skin.

To serve, spoon the sauce into the middle of a warm plate and place the fish on top, skin side up.

Bitter chocolate tart

Sea food and shellfish can be so deliciously light that there's always room for a good pudding. This recipe is a chocoholic's dream: crisp pastry with an unctuous truffle-like filling. Serve with a dollop of crème fraîche to cut through the richness of the dessert, or a handful of berries such as raspberries or strawberries.

Ingredients
1 tart shell (baked blind)
1 fl oz/25ml cognac
1 lb 8 oz/685g dark chocolate (Green and Blacks is delicious)
6 oz/170g unsalted butter
1 pt 5 fl oz/750ml double cream
Cocoa powder (for dusting)

Method
Break up the chocolate into small pieces and place in a bain-marie.* Once this is melted, stir in the butter and the cognac until the mixture is well blended. Remove bowl from the heat, add the double cream and mix well.

Pour this mixture into the tart shell and allow it to cool. The tart can be refrigerated at this point if it is not to be eaten immediately. Dust with cocoa powder just before serving. (Any surplus filling can be turned into truffles: just cool the mixture, shape into balls and roll in cocoa or chopped pecans.)

*A mixing bowl sitting in the mouth of a saucepan with simmering water will do just as well. The bowl must not touch the water.

Carole Fitzgerald

Carole Fitzgerald has always loved the sea and chose to study at St Andrews University primarily because of this. In the 1980s, along with a good friend, she renovated a shore-front building in South Queensferry and turned it into The Old Boathouse Restaurant, where she successfully established its reputation for focussing on local produce, particularly seafood.

The lack of shellfish at that time was a great frustration – her supplier was on the West Coast of Scotland and it was at this time that she first began to appreciate the relatively unexplored Argyll coast. Many of the places that feature in this book were family holiday spots back then and she is delighted that the area is now being recognised for its wonderful produce.

She is married with three children and, before she moved to Argyll, was the editor of an IT magazine in Glasgow.

Laura Thomson

Laura's love of photography was fuelled while working in France. Originally trained in traditional medium-format film, she loves working digitally, both in terms of the flexibility it offers and the ability to liaise closely and immediately with clients. Now a much sought after freelance photographer based in Glasgow, Laura's portfolio is extensive, and she has worked on shoots ranging from fashion to food to interiors.

Laura now believes herself to have the best of both worlds – a classically trained eye that seeks out the perfect shot, combined with the ability to immediately see the results, and gauge the client's reaction. Food has always been one of Laura's favourite passions and the opportunity to work with The Seafood Trail establishments has been one of her most memorable assignments: fabulous food, served in the most scenic of Scottish locations by people passionate about what they do.

Her work can be seen online at
www.Ltphotography.co.uk

Ann Kennedy

Ann Kennedy is a late starter to the world of photography, having graduated from college at the age of 43 with an Advanced Diploma in Illustrative Photography.

She specialises in black and white fine art land and seascape photography and works mainly in Scotland using 35mm and medium format SLR cameras and film. Much of Ann's inspiration for her unique work began in Kintyre, looking westwards over the islands of Gigha, Islay and Jura towards the Atlantic Ocean. The Kintyre peninsula is one of Ann's most loved places and her association with the area stretches as far back as her childhood holidays: the ever-changing skies and dramatic lighting, coupled with the wild beauty of the coastline, provides her with endless material.

Ann loves working with film and she uses textures and patterns together with atmospheric lighting to create moody, thought-provoking images which draw the eye to the finer detail and beauty of a landscape which might otherwise be overlooked. Part of the challenge is waiting for the right light, the right sky, the right mood – and she could happily wait all day for the sun to drop from the sky over Jura. 'I consider myself blessed to be able to pursue a vocation in such beautiful surroundings,' she says.

Details of where you can purchase copies of Ann's prints together with up-and-coming exhibitions feature on her websites:

www.annkennedyphotography.co.uk
www.annkennedyphoto.com

Weights and Measurements

When cooking, use either the imperial or metric equivalent. Do not mix the two methods together in the same recipe. Please note that conversions below are not exact equivalents.

Weights:

15g (½ oz)
30g (1 oz)
55g (2 oz)
85g (3 oz)
100g (3½ oz)
115g (4 oz)
140g (5 oz)
170g (6 oz)
200g (7 oz)
225g (8 oz)
300g (10½ oz)
340g (12 oz)
400g (14 oz)
450g (1 lb)
500g (1 lb 2 oz)
550g (1¼ lb)
600g (1 lb 5 oz)
675g (1½ lb)
800g (1¾ lb)
900g (2 lb)
1kg (2¼ lb)
1.25kg (2¾ lb)
1.5kg (3 lb 3 oz)
2kg (4½ lb)

Volume:

5ml (1 tsp)
10ml (2 tsp)
15ml (3 tsp or 1 tbs)
22ml (1½ tbs)
30ml (2 tbs)
45ml (3 tbs)
60ml (4 tbs or ¼ cup)
75ml (2½ fl oz)
90ml (3 fl oz)
100ml (3½ fl oz)
120ml (4 fl oz or ½ cup)
150ml (5 fl oz)
200ml (7 fl oz)
250ml (8½ fl oz or 1 cup)
300ml (10 fl oz)
360ml (12 fl oz)
400ml (14 fl oz)
450ml (15 fl oz)
500ml (17 fl oz exact)
600ml (1 pt)
750ml (1¼ pt)
900ml (1½ pt)
1L (2 pt)
1.5L (2¾ pt)
2L (3½ pt)

1 teaspoon (tsp) = 5ml
1 tablespoon (tbs) = 15ml

Notes

Notes

Notes

Notes

Notes